The Pocket Guide to Fishing

Copyright © 1999 Losange

Managing Editor: Hervé Chaumeton
Project Coordination: Myriam Weber
Design and Layout: Nathalie Lachaud, Jean-François Laurent, Isabelle Véret
Photography: Stéphanie Henry, Véronique Janvier, Chantal Mialon

Original title: Le mini-guide de la pêche

Copyright © 2000 for this English edition:
Könemann Verlagsgesellschaft mbH
Bonner Strasse 126, D-50968 Cologne

Translation from French: David Fry and John Trevor Williams in association with First Edition
Translation
Editing: Eelin Thomas in association with First Edition Translation
Typesetting: The Write Idea in association with First Edition Translation, Cambridge, UK
Project coordination: Nadja Bremse
Production: Ursula Schümer
Printing and binding: Star Standard Industries Ltd., Singapore

Printed in Singapore

ISBN 3-8290-4352-x

10 9 8 7 6 5 4 3 2 1

The Pocket Guide to Fishing

Pierre Affre
Pascal Durantel
Patrick Guillotte

CONTENTS

Introduction

A superb Norwegian salmon caught by casting on spinning tackle.

In the beginning was the worm. The start of the whole history of fishing could go like this: a worm on a hook, a hook attached to a line, the line fastened on a pole with, at its other end, a child. A child fishing with worm as bait in a stream, pool or pond, in a small or large river, no matter where. A child who disturbs the glassy surface of the water, sometimes to take out a fish, but with greater certainty to indulge in a daydream. The French author René Fallet wrote: "It is to myself that I owe this melancholic, almost absurdly desperate air: it has been perhaps only in the green pastures of running water and still water that I have known a few moments of that improbable thing, that carrot beyond our reach, that we persist in calling happiness." He further says: "Fishing is not difficult. It is real child's play, from the time when children used to play in grain lofts, in the days when they

existed. All it amounts to is water, a fish, and a man trying to catch that fish by means of a small steel hook. Let us not forget the love of fishing, for it is stronger than the bait."

The child grows up, and passion prevails over reason. The dream fades, becomes reality, and the worm may sometimes be replaced by a fly, a grasshopper, a cricket or a spoonbait.

Then, more than ever, hope is within grasp; hope that sometimes weighs a few grams, like a gleaming freshwater bleak, or tens of kilograms in the case of a wels catfish. Nevertheless, the story remains the same, and its opening words are: "In the beginning there was the prey." Who, however, or what, is the prey in this game of "catch-as-catch-can:" the one that takes the bait or the one who casts it? The float twitches as it drifts along with the current, bobbing through the ripples. A bite, what a magical

Introduction

moment! Fishing remains a real part of country life, with its rituals and its highs and lows, whether at the heart of the largest city or in the most desolate and isolated place. In the pages that follow you will discover, or rediscover, fishing with rod and line.

Browse through this profusely illustrated guide in search of the most modest cyprinid or the most formidable predator. What now follows is a comprehensive account of a favorite pastime, ranging from the most elementary techniques to the most sophisticated practices.

Dreams and adventures are catered for in the pages devoted to the fishes of the New World and of some renowned destinations in Europe and elsewhere. Explanatory diagrams will help you to assemble your tackle most efficiently at home or at the water's edge; the rest is then up to you!

The famous Bridge Pool at Ballina (Ireland), near the mouth of the River Moy; a mecca for salmon fishing booked up for years ahead! Note the wading stick used to keep one's balance in the currents.

The majestic action of the fly fisherman preparing to set down the artificial fly in a current.

SALMONIDAE, CHARS, EUROPEAN WHITEFISH (COREGONIDS)

Biology

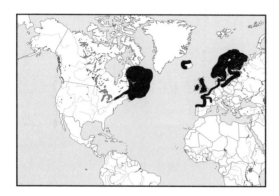

FOREIGN NAMES

French: saumon de l'Atlantique.
German: Lachs, Salm.
Norwegian: laks.
Spanish: salmon.

DESCRIPTION

The Atlantic salmon was the first member of the "trout" family described by Linnaeus. *Salmo*, if it was *salar* (not all authors agree on that), was derived from the Latin verb *salire*. When invading Gaul, Caesar's legionaries gave the name to the large fish, unknown where they came from (there are no salmon in the Mediterranean Basin), that they saw leaping in most large Northern European rivers that they had to cross. The Atlantic salmon is the type species of the family Salmonidae. Until some 40 years ago this family was taken to include such different fishes as trout, chars, coregonids, and even smelts. Chars are now included in the family

A fine winter salmon leaping in the falls of a French river, the Allagnon.

A school of superb Atlantic salmon going up a Norwegian river. The spawning grounds are near!

Thymallidae, whitefish in the Coregonidae, and smelts in the Osmeridae. Alongside the trout species (genus *Salmo*, with which, as we shall see, the Atlantic salmon is to be classed), the family Salmonidae includes Pacific salmon (genus *Oncorhynchus*), chars (genus *Salvelinus*), huchons (genus *Hucho*), lenoks (genus *Brachymystax*), and Ohrid trout (genus *Salmothymus*). Even when stripped of the chars, whitefish and smelts, the Salmonidae remain a very large family with more than 100 species, originally confined in distribution to the Northern Hemisphere. Many authors think, largely on paleontological, anatom-

ical as well as physiological grounds, that the Atlantic salmon is nothing other than a very large trout, a species closely akin to the sea trout or, as we shall see for "freshwater salmonids," lake trout.

Awareness of the different phases of the biological cycle lived through by these fish in the ocean and in fresh water gave rise over the centuries to the giving of common names, many of which have persisted. At the close of the 19th century many authors still maintained that salmon with elongated jaws ascending the river and salmon parr, which migrate downstream, were different

species. For adult fish, we shall use the terms: winter or large salmon, spring salmon and summer salmon (British term, grilse). Post-spawning fish are called kelts.

Parr is the term for juvenile fish, which subsequently develop into smolts.

GEOGRAPHIC DISTRIBUTION

The question that arises for the salmon, as for other migratory salmonids, is whether the fish was originally a marine species that became secondarily adapted to fresh water, essentially in search of a safer spawning environment, or whether the salmonids

Biology

Salmon leaping at "la Bajasse" on the River Allier (France).

were freshwater fishes that appeared on the scene more than two million years ago, and subsequently migrated into the sea in search of more abundant food. The latter hypothesis now appears to be the more widely accepted, and the great Ice Ages that began about one million years ago in the Northern Hemisphere were certainly a root cause of this passage from fresh to salt water. On melting, these enormous masses of ice appreciably reduced the salinity of the neighboring ocean waters, thus facilitating the passage from one environment to the other, which had become essential because of considerable reduction in the availability of food in the frozen rivers. Most fish certainly died, but some distant ancestors of the present-day trout,

salmon and chars arrived in the estuaries and ventured out into the high sea, where they found a relatively abundant food supply, at least during the summer. Given, however, that fresh water was what they were accustomed to, their mode of reproduction forced them to return to it in order to spawn, which gave rise to the migratory phenomenon. Most authors regard *Salmo salar* as the most likely common ancestor to have succeeded in making this adaptation. It would then have given rise not only to the various forms of trout, but also to the Pacific salmon, which became differentiated over a period of between 500,000 and one million years. In the North Atlantic, as the ice sheets repeatedly advanced and retreated,

Salmo salar ultimately took up residence on the northern shores which, on the American side, extend from the State of Maine to northern Labrador, and on the

Chum salmon spawning in an Alaskan river.

The Far North, where salmon fatten in the sea before returning to their native rivers to spawn.

European side from half way up the coast of Portugal to beyond the Kola Peninsula, in Russia. The limits usually given for the distribution of the species are from the River Minho, in Portugal, to the Pechora, the river that is a dividing line between European Russia and Siberia. On the American side, Cape Cod marks the southern limit, and to the north, in Ungava Bay, the River Leaf is the last to be visited. The wanderings of the salmon in salt water are not well known. All that has been known for about 50 years is that there are some feeding grounds where salmon born in different countries congregate at some time in their marine phase. The best known lies close to the west coast of Greenland, south of Davis Strait. The Irminger Sea, between the east coast of Greenland and Iceland, also seems to be a marine assembly area. Salmon from European and Canadian rivers are to be found in these areas. Norwegian, Scottish and, possibly, French salmon congregate around the Faeroe and Lofoten islands.

Furthermore, some scientists consider that the Faeroe islands are only an initial stage for many European salmon

A landlocked salmon, the North American ouananiche (Sebago salmon).

Biology

found all along the Greenland route. The North Atlantic undoubtedly still has secrets to give up. Lastly, the Baltic provides sea-grazing for Russian, Finnish, and Swedish salmon, which find such a congenial environment in its waters, with their rich food supply and low salinity, that they do not seek to leave. These Baltic salmon, which reach record weights (Berg cites a 102-lb [46.5-kg] fish caught at Leningrad, in the mouth of the Neva), are closely akin to the "freshwater salmon" found in the large Swedish, Russian and Finnish lakes, left over from the last Ice Ages. On the American side, the term "landlocked" is used for such salmon, also deprived of access to the sea by glacial moraines. The ouananiches, in Quebec, and the Sebago salmon, in

Norwegian fjord opening on the sea.

ATLANTIC SALMON *(Salmo salar)*

Maine, are cases in point. The whole life cycle is lived out in fresh water, with adult fish feeding in the lakes (lake-grazing) on such fodder fish as whitefish, smelt and bleak, and migrating back up the tributaries in the autumn to spawn.

BEHAVIOR

We have all heard of the wonderful story of the little salmon born in the river, where it grows during its youth, but one fine day gets the urge to go off to Greenland and become the magnificent fish we know, and which will inevitably return to reproduce in the river of its birth. Wonderful as it may seem, this story is true. In particular, the return of the salmon, not only to the river, but also to the pool where it was born some

three, four, or five years previously is now well established.

From parr to adult salmon

Whether it be in Quebec, Norway, Scotland or France, the cycle of the Atlantic salmon, *Salmo salar*, has several distinct phases (at least three), separated in time and space. An initial exclusively freshwater phase, which could be termed youth, followed by a marine feeding stage, and ending in a phase of return to fresh water, or the reproductive phase. The little salmon, initially an alevin, has to be born in fresh water on a bed of stones cleaned by the parent fish before they lay their eggs. These first months of life will be identical to those of young troutlings born at the same time. A keen observer

The eggs are laid on a stony bed.

may note that these young parr, as they are called, are more voracious and active than the others. In the upper reaches of the watercourse they consume large quantities of insects drifting on the surface or found in the larval stage between the stones on the bottom, along with other small invertebrates (worms, crustaceans, mollusks). After one or more often two years of this regime they have become magnificent small fish, from 6 to 10 inches (15 to 25 cm) or more in length, already well versed in battling against the strongest currents. Then, one fine day, or more likely one fine night, when the moon changes phase, most often in May, a great transformation alters the whole course of their life. The parr undergo smoltification, i.e. hormonal changes bring about a real metamorphosis that will change their form and their mode of life. Whereas it was difficult before to dis-

The juvenile salmon, or parr, resembles a trout.

Biology

THE DANGERS OF LIFE IN THE OCEAN

The greatest causes of mortality, due especially to cold and lack of food, are found in the sea. More than 80% of the salmon caught or scientifically followed in the marine feeding grounds along the Greenland coast or around the Faeroes are in water layers between 39 and 50 °F (4 to 10 °C). According to scientists, the greenhouse effect and the heating of the atmosphere noted in recent years could affect salmon very adversely during their marine phase and, by melting the polar ice cap, this could cool the surface waters in this region, which would force the salmon to move southwards in search of warmer waters. The preferred prey of the salmon might not be so abundant in those zones, and the potential predators, seals, killer whales, sharks, could be far more plentiful and active. The ban on hunting seal pups in the ice-fields over the last 15 or so years has increased the gray seal population in the North Atlantic to more than two million. Given that one seal can consume up to 66 pounds (30 kg) of salmon a day, the effect on wild salmon stocks can readily be imagined.

Professional net fishing is making great inroads into salmon populations.

tinguish them from young trout because they were so similar in shape and coloration, within a few days they acquire the uniformly silver livery found primarily in dwellers in a salt-water environment (sardines, sprats), and their bodies become longer. They are preparing to leave the gravelly and stony bottoms

Radio-tracking of salmon on the Haut Allier (France).

where they were born to move as a body into the open water in the middle of the river and descend to the estuary. The profound physiological changes connected with "smoltification" will enable them to be as at ease in salt water as in sea water and, within a few hours or, at most, a few days of becoming accustomed to their new marine environment, they will leave home shores for the great crossing of the Atlantic to arrive off Green-land – for it is in the cold, food-rich waters of the icy Arctic Ocean that most European salmon are genetically programmed to grow. There they will remain for one to three years on average, feeding actively day and night in the shoals of sprats, herring, squid, and prawns that abound in these latitudes, until they become the magnificent fish known to us. Then, one day, a mysterious but urgent call makes them forsake these marine feeding

WHY ARE SALMON GETTING SMALLER AND SMALLER?

Research has shown that salmon in waters that are slightly warmer, even by as little as half a degree, become sexually mature far quicker. This would explain why, since about ten years ago, more and more of the salmon returning in most countries where there are salmon runs are small fish, known as grilse, and why there are everywhere slightly fewer large salmon that have spent two or three winters in the sea. The grilse which, by definition, have spent one year in the sea, are also getting smaller. In Scotland, for example, their average weight has fallen from 6 to 5 pounds (3–2½ kg) over the last twenty years. Grilse of less than three pounds have been caught in many rivers of the British Isles and Iceland. It could also be that over time the many salmon hatcheries have helped to debase the wild race.

Biology

The male ready to spawn develops a hook, the kype.

Reproduction

grounds to return to their rivers of birth to reproduce.

Just as surely as, two or three years before, they set out from Saint-Nazaire for Greenland, they will regain the Loire estuary after a 2,500 mile (4,000 km) crossing. Then they will ascend the great river to its confluence with the Allier, the river in which they will continue their quest until they find the stony bottom where they were born five or six years earlier. There they will stay in the deepest places in the river awaiting the spawning time, which is between mid November and late December, depending on the locality. The salmon fast throughout this return journey in fresh water. Only the reserves of fat and protein built up at sea enable the fish to move up the rivers and to wait, sometimes for months (up to a year for some fish that entered the rivers very early on), before spawning. This lengthy fast and the difficulties and obstacles encountered on the voyage explain why a salmon that weighed more than 22 pounds (10 kg) in the Loire estuary will weigh no more than 13 or 15 pounds (6 or 7 kg) on arrival in the spawning grounds in the Haut-Allier and little more than about 11 pounds (5 kg) following spawning. Spent salmon are called kelts (in France vultures, *charognards*, because of their somewhat wretched appearance). They are all skin and bones and are, in appearance, so different from the magnificent creatures that they were at the start of the ascent, that they were thought for centuries not to be the same fish.

Having completed their reproductive task, they are so physically rundown that almost all are doomed to die. However, a few will find the strength to swim to a spot sheltered from the current, there to recuperate, for they do recover their appetite after spawning. Should the winter not be too harsh, the survivors will go down to the ocean in the spring, and make a second voyage to the food-rich waters off Greenland. Subsequently, they will return

Setting a net in an estuary: death to the salmon!

Demolition of a dam to help salmon return.

to spawn once again, infallibly to the waters where they were born. Very occasionally, salmon born in small watercourses along the coast, in which the spawning grounds are fairly close to the estuary, may return to fresh water as many as three times.

THE SEA-FEEDING STAGE

Even today, very little is known about the marine stage in the life of salmon. Tagging trials, using pressure-sensitive probes, conducted in the feeding grounds around the Faeroe Isles, have permitted the tracking of tagged salmon for several days, and have shown that these fish are capable of diving rapidly to more than 500 feet (150 m) and of coming back up nearly as quickly. They would appear to hunt actively during the day at a depth of about 130 feet (40 m), whereas at night, rising with their prey, they more readily spend their time between the surface and a depth of less than 30 feet (10 m). Studies of stomach contents, conducted off Greenland, have shown that, depending on the season, they contain small fish, crustaceans and mollusks. Northern prawns, which are naturally red, figure largely in their diet, along with small squid. The fish prey most frequently found are herrings, sprats, capelin (a kind of smelt), sand lances, and young cod. These fodder fish, most of which are very oily, enable salmon to gain up to one pound (½ kg) a month during the fine season, when surface temperatures reach 46 °F (8 °C). We can expect that, after two years in Greenland waters, a salmon will have put on 13–18 pounds (6–8 kg). At the end of their third sea winter, salmon weigh between 22 and 27 pounds (10 or 12 kg); the record fish of 33 to 44 pounds (15 to 20 kg) have usually spent a longer period of approximately four years in the sea.

Fishing techniques

The Atlantic salmon, the king of fish, is undoubtedly the species that most arouses the passions of anglers, who will travel the world seeking it out.

FEEDING HABITS OF THE SALMON

Fishing for salmon with rod and line differs from fishing for all other species, in that it is a fish that does not feed in the river. Salmon returning to fresh water fast, derive their energy from the vast reserves of fat and protein accumulated during their sea life. Fishermen have always been intrigued by the fact that adult salmon running upstream do not feed in the rivers, and some assert that if the stomach of caught fish is always empty, the reason is because the hooked fish had time to regurgitate previously swallowed prey during the fight. Scientists now tell us that, on returning to fresh water, *Salmo salar* is physiologically incapable of feeding, even should it so desire.

The cells of the gastric mucosa and the digestive glands have become so atrophied as to cease functioning. Consequently, when a salmon seizes one of our lures or baits, it has not been prompted by hunger, but rather by the fact that its only way of examining the intrusive object more closely

A fine catch by whip casting.

is to take hold of it in that way. Animal behaviorists who study this fish speak of reactions of aggressiveness or curiosity, of annoyance, or the instinct to play. But there might also be some memory of the oceanic banquets off Greenland that, in the space of two or three years of a high-calorie diet, transform the small salmon of scarcely one ounce (30 g) on leaving the river into a magnificent fish of 22, 26 or 33 pounds (10, 12 or 15 kg). While it is probable that the obvious pulsations of a large wobbling spoonbait, the rapid rotation of a Devon minnow, or a scarlet prawn entering the field of vision may cause an "aggressive"

Fly fishing, using a two-handed rod, in a Norwegian river.

The salmon often bites in the twilight hours.

snap of the jaws, it is more often curiosity or play that will make a large salmon leave its lie, often several yards away, to take a small fly crossing the pool at a depth of two fingers beneath the surface. On other occasions, it is certainly through curiosity or irritation that a salmon, located and "bombarded" for several hours with the same, or different lures, will ultimately "bite" as the lure passes over its head for the umpteenth time. Lastly, you will have difficulty persuading an angler using a worm, that the salmon, which has swallowed his "earthworm cluster" so deeply that he cannot get back his hook, did not have a small hole to fill, even if physiologically unable to digest the offering. The prawn also undoubtedly triggers a reflex of feeding type in the large migratory fish, the starting point for which should undoubtedly be sought in the salmon's fantastic olfactory memory. William Calderwood, a former Scottish Salmon Fisheries Inspector, undoubtedly one of the most serious students of salmon behavior, held the view that if the salmon takes worms, it is because it regards them as delicacies, just as some of us may feel about oysters, or that a fine, wriggling offering of earthworms could remind *Salmo salar* of the small squid that it enjoyed in the ocean.

CHOICE OF LURE

Be that as it may, the whole art of a good salmon fisherman will consist in preferring some particular lure or bait on the basis of the assumed "mood" of the fish at a given time and in a given place. A fish newly arrived from the ocean will not be tackled in the same way as one that has been present in the pool for several weeks and thus has different tastes.

The boldest "biters" are always salmon newly arrived from salt water. At the end of the season, after a long stay in fresh water, when the fish are assembled in the area of the spawning grounds, what prompts a salmon to "bite"

Fishing techniques

Atlantic salmon lies in a pool

will be very different from the motives of the same fish a few months before, in the lower reaches. In the reproductive zone, the fish will bite to defend a territory which will also be that of its future mate. Nor should we forget that the salmon is a great traveler and that its ascent to the headwaters of the streams and rivers is conditioned by the state of their waters. A drop in water level and the warming of the water in summer will make the fish take up a position at the very bottom of a hole, where it will be quite difficult to rouse from its lethargy.

On the other hand, a flood following several weeks of low water level will lower the temperature and the salmon will head into the current and take an interest in our lures. Knowledge of the water level for each pool will be a key factor influencing how it is fished. The secret of the success of a great salmon fisherman is to be found in this knowledge of water levels and fish lies. That is why, whatever your expertise in the various techniques of salmon fishing, it is often essential, when you arrive at an unknown river, to have the assistance of a *ghillie* (a Gaelic word meaning male servant or attendant). Learn how to listen to him, for his advice will be most invaluable; he will not look on you as a competitor, but will be genuinely delighted with your success, as what he earns is indeed largely dependent on your gratitude. On Scottish, Irish and also Norwegian rivers, ghillies could be said to be a part of the scenery, and are themselves

Superb brace of salmon caught on the Ponoï, in Russia.

Large cock salmon caught by spinning in a Norwegian fjord.

mostly excellent fishermen. Having initially followed their expert advice and tried out all the various lures and patterns of flies recommended, there is, however, nothing to prevent you from trying other ones, if you have not had any results. One pass with a lure or a bait that is not usually used on a river, may sometimes "rouse" a large salmon, and prompt the long-awaited bite.

CASTING

It is often believed that very special, costly equipment is needed for salmon fishing. However, since the advent of carbon fiber, any good 9 to 11 ft (2.7 to 3.3 m) rod with a modern monofilament line of .32 or .37 mm diameter (12 lb/5.4 kg to 15 lb/6.8 kg breaking strength) is perfectly suit-able on large rivers at the start of the season.

When water levels are high, you will possibly need something more robust, but the wide variety of salmon rods available are affordable. On these major watercourses your reel will need at least 165 yd (150 m) of .40 or .42 mm-diameter line giving a breaking strength of 18 lb/8kg to 20 lb/9 kg, which will hold a much heavier fish.

Wobbling spoonbaits

Elongated models of the Toby type, weighing about ½–1 oz (15–30 g), are among the most widely used lures at the beginning of the fishing season, especially on large rivers.

They are quite easy to use. No weight-ing is needed with wobblers, which are easy to cast and to maintain in the current as they drift. In cold waters and strong currents they should be worked as close to the bottom as possible. Many specialists prefer large light wobblers, which are more difficult to cast, but which "react" better to the currents and therefore swim more freely.

The main drawback of these spoons is the large number of "failures" that they occasion, not, as has often been written, because the salmon bears down on the spoon part to free itself, but because the jerky, revolving, irregular and

Fishing techniques

unpredictable movement of the spoon (which makes it attractive to the fish) often has the result that it is taken badly, and rarely along the axis, as are Devon minnows.

Revolving spoons

These spoons are used mainly in small coastal watercourses, in which they have now replaced small Devon minnows.

Devon minnows

Many salmon fishermen still prefer these lures, despite their disadvantages, the foremost of which is that they twist the line. There are sev-

eral reasons for this preference: the considerable weight of Devon minnows for their small volume, at least for metallic models, means that they cast well and fish deeply, as is often necessary with salmon, but above all their rapid rotation appears to exert an attraction that other lures do not have. Lastly, "fishing in line," they are generally well swallowed, and after the strike very few fish get off the hook, as compared with the use of wobblers, for example. The Devon minnow is also a lure widely used by salmon fishermen in the British Isles. British Devons are of turned wood, and are therefore very light. Their main disad-

vantage is that the line has to be leaded at a distance of about 2 to 2½ feet (60 to 80 cm), which makes them less easy to cast than a copper or brass Devon. However, as regards the action of the spoon, that drawback

Traditional French Devon of mountain torrents and the Allier, with its "pajamas."

becomes an advantage, because their lightness makes them highly maneuverable, a little like a fly, and responsive to the slightest vagaries of the current. Even when reeled in very slowly, which is very important for cold waters, or merely maintained broadside to the current, they will have less tendency to catch on the moss-covered rocks on the bottom, because their natural tendency to float will make them lift a good 4

Acrobatic leap, or "tailer" on the Sainte-Marguerite (Quebec).

inches (10 cm) above the lead. As with any type of Devon, there should always be a good swivel between the body and the end of the line to keep the line from kinking.

Swimming fish

Although spoons and Devon minnows are the main lures used for salmon fishing, there is nothing to stop you from trying others. Swimming fish of the Rapala type, 2–2½ inches (5–9 cm) long, give excellent results and are greatly used in Scandinavia.

Some plugs (Abu Kynoch) give good results on Scottish rivers. This swimming fish model is certainly responsible for more than half the salmon catches on the Tay in pools fished from a small boat (the harling technique).

Dead fish

In expert hands, a good minnow, a gudgeon or, better still, a loach, presented across pools on a Rhodoid mount, is undoubtedly among the best salmon traps, but this is illegal now in the United States, Great Britain, and many other countries.

On public rivers, if this

A fine Icelandic salmon taken with a swimming fish bait.

method is permitted and where metallic lures are used daily, this natural bait often makes the difference.

Worms

Worm, usually several together, is used in France almost exclusively at the beginning of the season, when rivers are high or in

Worm fishing is most effective when the water is high.

spate. Many fish that have been "aroused" by a spoon, or held for a few seconds before getting off the hook, are subsequently tried, often successfully, with worm, persisted with for several days in the same place. The bundle of worms is positioned in an eddy, close to the bank where a salmon is known to be lying, and then comes the wait to see if it will bite. Real worm fishing, which is particularly productive, as practiced by specialists in large running rivers, involves "rolling" fishing, a little like the trout in a torrent. The feel of the salmon

Fishing techniques

taking the worms is very stirring. What happens initially is that the bait simply stops moving, followed by some very distinct tugs, due to the movements of the jaws of the salmon, which usually remains chewing for several seconds, and then, if you are patient, the movement of the fish up stream. That is the time to strike. A salmon taken on worm is unlikely to come off the hook when being played, but the line must always be strong enough for the fish to be landed, even among the submerged roots where it took the bait.

Prawn

This bait is so highly thought of that its use is prohibited in many places. Because of its fragility, the prawn is a difficult bait to use in rivers littered with tree branches or water weeds. A new prawn must be used after each attempt, and they are costly. This problem does not arise on canalized rivers or on stony bottoms in strong currents; as soon as the water warms a little, say when it it reaches 48–50 °F (9–10 °C), salmon are rarely indifferent to this bait, even should hundreds of metal lures

have passed before their eyes. Even if they fail to gulp down the passing prawn, salmon react to it and thus indicate their presence to the fisherman, either by a surface eddy, or by leaping right out of the water soon after it passes. Pink prawns, preferably bunched, are preserved in glycerin and mounted at the end of the line after having been straightened and threaded on a strand of piano wire. They should be secured to the mount by fine copper wire or elastic thread. Leading the line at least a yard (1 m) from the prawn is generally recommended.

FLY-FISHING

Contrary to what many trout fisherman think, fly-fishing for salmon is really very easy. Better than that: after only a few days' practice, even in the first year, it is quite possible to make a magnificent fish rise and catch it.

In practice, two-handed fly casting is easier to learn than casting with one hand. Especially with the modern materials now available (carbon fiber and plastic self-floating lines). The fishing technique itself is extremely

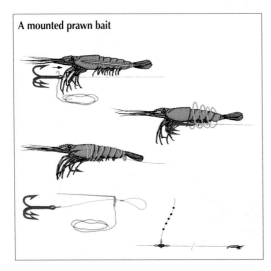

A mounted prawn bait

Fly-fishing at the head of a pool where salmon often bite the most.

simple: a wet fly is cast three-quarters downstream toward the opposite bank, then left to describe an arc in the current of the water.

Equipment

If you are making your first attempts on a small river you will find a 12-foot (3.7 m) rod and a no. 9 line quite sufficient. For those already experienced in wet-fly trout fishing with single-handed rods 9–11 feet long (2.8–3.4 m), will find their experience suitable. Provision should also be made for a line tapering to a leader between .28–.30 mm diameter at the tip. On large rivers, you should have a rod at least 15 feet (4.6 m) long and a no. 10 to no. 12 line. Only this large "gear" will enable you to

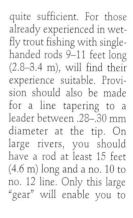

A fine Quebec Atlantic salmon, about to be ringed.

Fishing techniques

North American fisherman prefer a single-handed rod for fly-fishing.

reach the opposite bank without too much physical exertion on such large rivers.

Fishing action

Deciding when to strike or rather when not to strike is the greatest difficulty that faces a novice salmon fisherman. When wet-fly trout fishing, the strike must be made immediately the artificial fly is felt to be touched. This is a reflex that must be unlearned with salmon fishing. The best technique is still to leave the line free from the reel. When the strike is made, the salmon will easily take up several turns that will

enable it to turn round, and it will generally be well hooked when you react. In our opinion, the choice of fly is fairly unimportant by comparison with the manner of presentation. There are thousands of different patterns of the traditional Anglo-Saxon tied fly in which feathers are used. Nowadays, the best specialists from Scotland to Quebec, also taking in Iceland and the rivers of Russian Karelia, exclusively use flies tied with the hair of badgers, squirrels, and other mam-

Rather proud of his catch!

mals. There are, however, three main principles that we think should be respected: First principle: pale shades of flies for bright weather. Second principle: the higher the water temperature and the closer to 64 or 66 °F (18 or 19 °C), and the lower and clearer the water (conditions that usually go together), the smaller the fly should be. Third and most basic principle: the best fly will always be the one in the water.

Ireland is still a destination of choice for salmon.

Biology

DESCRIPTION

Pacific salmon were given the name by the first British settlers in British Columbia because the forms and mode of life of these fish were similar to those of *Salmo salar* in their country of origin. The generic name *Oncorhynchus*, (which means hook nose, a reference to the upper jaw of these fish,

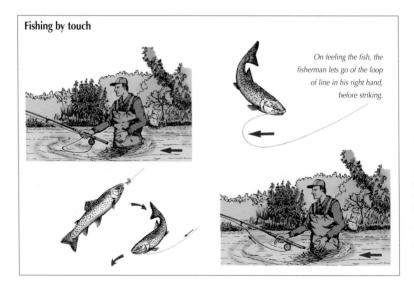

Fishing by touch

On feeling the fish, the fisherman lets go of the loop of line in his right hand, before striking.

PACIFIC SALMON *(Oncorhynchus)*

which curves downward in a hook as spawning time approaches), has been applied since 1741 to five Pacific salmon species described by the German naturalist, Wilhelm Steller, who accompanied Vitus Bering on his first voyage to explore the eastern seaboard of the Pacific (commissioned by the Russian empress, Catherine the Great). That explains why the species names of all Pacific salmon are phonetic renderings of the Russian names of these fish, previously known from the eastern seaboard of Asiatic Siberia. Thus, *tshawytscha* is the vernacular name given to the chinook by the inhabitants of Kamchatka. The same holds for *nerka*, *kisutch*, *keta*, and *gorbusha* which are Russian, or more correctly Siberian, names

Superb king salmon (chinook) caught by spinning on the River Karluk (Kodiak-Alaska).

Durham Ranger.

Light colored fly for clear water.

Dark fly for turbid water.

SALMONIDAE 33

Biology

Freshly caught red salmon, taken by fly on the River Kenaï (Alaska).

for the other four species found on the American coast. On the Asiatic coast, of both Siberia and Japan, there are two further species: *Oncorhynchus masou*, and *Oncorhynchus biwa*. Since 1989, we must add to this list of Pacific salmon the rainbow trout, hereafter called *Oncorhynchus mykiss*. Many authors and paleontologists consider that *Oncorhynchus* species are the most recent to appear and therefore the most evolved (although most inevitably die after spawning). Their ancestor would undoubtedly have been a distant *Salmo*, and the differentiation would have appeared after the

separation, several hundred thousand years ago, of the American and Asiatic groups. The link for the transition from *Salmo* to *Oncorhynchus* is undoubtedly to be sought in one of the two Japanese species (*masou* or *biwa*) which, like *Salmo salar*, and unlike the other Pacific salmon, do not systematically die after the first spawning.

Pacific salmon in the ocean are magnificent fish, powerful in form, and perfectly spindle-shaped. Like most large predatory pelagic fishes (tuna, marlin, etc.), their back is a steely blue-gray, lightening on the flanks, and the belly is silvery white. Numerous black spots on the back extend from the top of the head to the tail. On arriving

in fresh water, these colors rapidly tarnish and, as spawning approaches, and depending on the species, they take on a livery ranging from brick-red to dead-leaf chestnut brown, or rich dark red. As with almost all salmonids, males are darker and more strongly colored than females.

Chinook salmon, *Oncorhynchus tshawytscha*, reach the greatest size, and there are many French salmon fishermen who fly out every summer to Alaska or British Columbia to pit themselves against fish that commonly weigh 30, 40, or even 50 or 60 pounds (13–27 kg). The largest chinook caught (netted) and officially weighed tipped the scales at 126

Four silvers, taken by fly.

As spawning time approaches, the male pink salmon is recognizable by its humped back.

pounds, or 57 kg, and was 4 feet 11 inches (1.52 m) long. The current record for rod and line is a fish of 97 pounds (44 kg) caught in the River Kenaï (Alaska) in 1985.

GEOGRAPHIC DISTRIBUTION

These salmon are migratory throughout the North Pacific, and may possibly venture through the Bering Strait into the icy Arctic Ocean. Their sea-feeding grounds also take them into the Sea of Japan and the Sea of Okhotsk.

In the rivers, they are found on the American coast from the latitude of southern California to Cape Hope, in Alaska, on the other side of the Bering Strait. On the Asiatic coast, they ascend the rivers from the latitude of Hokkaido (the northernmost island of Japan) to Anadyr Bay, in Siberia.

Nowadays, following numerous introductions, it is mainly coho and king (chinook) salmon that are found in the South Pacific around New Zealand, off the coast of Chile and even in the Antarctic. At the

beginning of the 19th century, acclimatization trials were held all over the place, including the Mediterranean. Chinook smolts, reared in the Trocadéro Aquarium, were released into the River Aude, the Rhône, the Var, and many small Corsican coastal streams. The adults (if the smolts grew) seem to have disappeared without trace in a sea that was certainly too warm and too saline. On the other hand, following release of juveniles in the Seine, adults weighing more than 22 pounds (10

Biology

The very short River Karluk — Kodiak Island, Alaska — affords the opportunity of catching fresh, completely white king (chinook).

Only a few fish in every thousand get lost and enter other watercourses. As they approach the coast, it is thanks to their fantastic sense of smell that the fish find the estuary, then the tributary and, ultimately, the pool where they emerged from the gravel bed between three and eight years previously. In the ocean their migrations may be as lengthy as 12,000 miles (18,000 km).

Reproduction
Depending on the river, the

Silver (coho) salmon in nuptial livery.

kg) were recaptured two or three years later in the Andelle and the Seine itself, below the navigation barrages. However, whereas the New Zealanders and the Chileans were more serious and persistent with their acclimatization trials, no returns of chinooks or cohos into French waters have been known for some considerable time.
In the 70s, the Americans were spectacularly successful in acclimatizing king and coho salmon in their Great Lakes (Michigan and Erie). The results were far beyond all expectations and, for about 30 years

now, hundreds of thousands of magnificent salmon, grown almost as large as in the sea, have been caught every year by sport fishermen, either by trolling in the lakes, or when the fish return to spawn in the rivers.

BEHAVIOR
Migration
Pacific salmon spend from one to six years (kings) in the ocean before returning to spawn and die in the river of their birth. The homing instinct to return to the river of birth is as good in this species as in *Salmo salar*, i.e. more than 99 per cent.

PACIFIC SALMON *(Oncorhynchus)*

spawning zones are between a few miles above the brackish zone and more than 1,330 miles (2,000 km) from the estuary, as was previously the case in the Columbia River. The features of spawning are very similar in pattern in all species to those of the Atlantic salmon. The female hollows out the redd and the eggs are no sooner fertilized than they are covered with coarse gravel and pebbles. Depending on the temperature, they will take 7 to 12 weeks to hatch. The alevins, which have a yolk sac (like *Salmo salar*), will remain for two to three weeks under the protective gravel. In the week following hatching, the adults are doomed to die in a state of advanced dilapidation. This sad end may be seen as an evolutionary adaptation of the species. In many Alaskan rivers, by virtue of harsh climatic conditions and the rock-strewn bottom, the aquatic invertebrate fauna is extremely scanty; but for the thousands of carcasses of parent fish rotting on the stones, there would not be any nutriment to start the food chain leading to the growth of the parr to adulthood.

Chum, or dog salmon, taken on fly in a river frequented by many bears, as is shown by the personal protection device ("bear scarer") carried in the fishing jacket.

In fresh water, juveniles feed mainly on insects. In the sea, migrating adults pursue schools of herring, smelts and Pacific anchovies, and also squid. Prawns also figure prominently in their diet.

Fishing techniques

Salmon of Pacific strains undoubtedly take flies less readily than their Atlantic counterparts. Even so, if you fish when the level is right (near low water) you can succeed.

French fishermen who have fished for king, coho, and pink salmon in Alaska and in British Columbia have found that the techniques used for Atlantic salmon give very good results, at least for casting. In fact, as for *Salmo salar*, the longer chinook salmon have been in fresh water, the more important it becomes to seek to arouse their curiosity or aggressiveness, to incite them to bite, than to gamble on an awakening of their feeding behavior. The matter is different in salt or brackish water, and Americans fish mainly from boats

Shrimp, streamer imitating a prawn.

This chum took a fly imitating a cluster of eggs.

Typically American wobbling spoon for salmon.

Red salmon, caught by spinning, using a spoon.

in the immense fjords known as sounds, where the fish continue to feed actively before entering the rivers flowing into them. The most successful technique of all is to tow herring or a herring and spoon combination at various depths in the wake of the fishing boat.

Kings and cohos (the main species sought by sportsmen) are in their best form at that time, both combative and receptive to food. Once they have entered fresh water, their condition declines rapidly, so that, after a few weeks, they can offer little more opposition than their weight at the end of the line. However, as they are often found in large rivers with strong currents, the fight that they put up at the end of a .45 mm-diameter line (breaking strength 18 lb/8 kg) may last a long time, although it cannot be compared with that of a fish that has only recently entered the estuary. Sinking lines are recommended for fly fishing, because chinook will show interest only in flies drifting at their depth, unlike Atlantic salmon, which will still rise to the surface after a fly, even after having spent several months in the river.

Biology

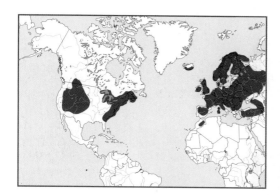

FOREIGN NAMES

French: *truite commune.*
German: *Forelle, Bachforelle.*
Spanish: *trucha.*

BROWN TROUT *(Salmo trutta fario)*

The attractive livery of the brown trout, with its characteristic red spots.

DESCRIPTION

The first written mention of the word trout in French (*truite*, written at the time *truitte*), appeared in 1555, in the book by Pierre Belon of Mans, *La nature et diversité des poissons avec leurs pourtraicts representez au plus près du naturel* (The nature and diversity of fish, with their portraits rendered as closely as possible to nature). It describes the trout earlier called the salar and the salmon trout, or sea trout. The name trout would be derived from the Latin *tructa* which, according to Vavon, who gives Sir Herbert Maxwell as his authority, itself came from the Greek *Troktes*, roughly translatable as voracious. That would

make the trout the embodiment of a voracious fish. Anyone who has seen a trout pursuing a school of minnows, taking great bites at them, will clearly recognize one of the essential character traits of the species. Valenciennes and Cuvier, who succeeded Lacépède in the French Natural History Museum, gave the handsome speckled fish the Latin name *Salmo ferox* (ferocious trout).

From among the many scientific names that ichthyologists have used to designate the trout, *Salmo variabilis*, now obsolete, was undoubtedly the most realistic. Few fish exhibit such variety of dimensions, livery and behavior as the

brown trout. That fact had already been recorded by Lacépède, who stated that "in the Department of *Seine-Inférieure* alone, different rivers are known to contain seven or eight varieties of trout that differ in color, spots, etc." The same holds in comparison of the morphology and livery of trout from different regions.

In general the back, sides and opercula (gill covers) are generally strewn with round or cross-shaped black spots of various sizes. The well-known red spots may or may not be present, may be small, large or "blown up" (in the Corsican trout), picked out in blue (ocellate, and sometimes aureolate).

Biology

Also in currents.

The color of the back ranges from black to light green, with intermediate shades of bluish gray and all shades of brown in some strains or races. The sides may be silvery, pearly, golden or yellowish. The belly, lastly, is white, or yellow, or any of the whole range of blends of these two colors. The fins range from yellow, through

Take care over presentation when dealing with a fish as wary as the trout!

shades of brown, to gray. In the course of an evolution of hundreds of thousands of years, every region, and even at times every river, has seen the development of trout varieties or races that have become its own, and that are, above all, perfectly adapted. The great polymorphism of the species is conditioned by the nature of the soil, by altitude, and by the gradient of the watercourse, the temperature range, the kind of food available, and a good many other factors. We must not, however, let ourselves be deceived by this extreme diversity, primarily manifested in dimensions, forms and liveries: river or brook

trout *Salmo trutta fario*, lake trout *Salmo trutta lacustris*, and finally sea trout *Salmo trutta trutta* are no more than what scientists now call "ecological forms" of what is ultimately one and the same fish: the brown trout.

GEOGRAPHICAL DISTRIBUTION

Consequently, we find trout throughout Europe, and in parts of the Mahgreb and Asia Minor, from Iceland (which has a fauna linking it to the Eurasian continent) to Afghanistan, passing en route through Scandinavia and the British Isles, in the north, and the Mediterranean Basin (including North Africa), in the south of the region.

BROWN TROUT *(Salmo trutta fario)*

The brown trout, which is our particular concern, and which must be said to have had a marine ancestor (sea trout), has moved out of the Atlantic, the English Channel, the North Sea and the Baltic to colonize the interior of the lands and islands whose shores are washed by those waters. Its penetration toward the headwaters was undoubtedly originally limited solely by the length of the river networks and by the insurmountable falls cutting across them.

All ichthyologists now concur in recognizing that the marine ancestor has given rise all over the place to landlocked or "sedentary" forms. It was, in the main, at the end of the last Ice Age that these differentiations occurred.

It has to be admitted that the trout of the Rhodanian Basin and of other Mediterranean river basins, which remain well individualized, had as their ancestor the marine *macrostigma* form, which must have frequented Mediterranean waters before they became too warm, well before the Quaternary glaciation. It is only for this subspecies that sedentary forms have survived to the present day.

Whereas the trout (*Salmo truttta labrax*) of the basins that discharge into the North Sea are merely subspecies of *Salmo trutta trutta*, the trout of the inland Caspian Sea, on the contrary, are a quite distinct

The trout is a typical denizen of clear, well-oxygenated running water. This cool mountain torrent is a fine example of its biotope.

species, very similar to some of the Swedish and Russian landlocked varieties of Atlantic salmon. Some ichthyologists treat these Caspian trout as highly differentiated Atlantic salmon. In support of their theory, these scientists point out that the Caspian was linked before the last Ice Age to the

White Sea, and through it to the icy Arctic Ocean, through the "intercepted" courses of the Volga (in the south), the Dvina and the Pechora (in the north). Along the latter rivers, which are still frequented

by *Salmo salar*, salmon from the Atlantic could have found their way into the Caspian Sea, and subsequently have found themselves trapped. Present-day genetic analyses could have confirmed or invalidated this theory, but unfortunately these enormous Caspian "trout" have now disappeared, owing to

Trout with large orange spots caught in Corsica: undoubtedly a macrostigma!

damming, overfishing, and pollution. In Asia, do Afghan trout still survive in the rivers of the Pamir? It is regrettable that, more than a century ago, the British introduced trout from the Thames Basin into these waters, and they have certainly hybridized with them. In Yugoslavia, but especially in Italy, the populations of marbled trout, that had come close to extinction, are now the object of programs for their protection and restoration in a number of watercourses.

It appears that *macrostigma*, especially the Corsican strain, has disappeared owing to the fish farming and other stocking operations carried out on a large scale for more than half a century with hatchery-reared fish of continental strains (most often the Atlantic and Danish strains). Similarly, in Morocco, it would appear that poorly considered introductions of metropolitan trout by zealous officers of the Forestry Commission at the time of the Protectorate, may have wiped out *macrostigma* in

most of its biotopes in the Atlas ranges. Nor would the situation appear to be very good in Sardinia and Sicily, where there is shameless poaching, but there are a few remote and fairly inaccessible streams in these two islands where the subspecies may have survived. What remains in the other European countries of the indigenous races of *fario*, whose great genetic variability created the wealth of the European salmon and trout heritage?

Half a century of ill-considered restocking operations, euphemistically called fish farming, but which are in fact nothing more than the dumping of degenerate and almost invariably diseased trout from fish farms, have wiped out most of the wild stocks through genetic regression and the transmission of infectious agents (viruses, bacteria and parasites). Researchers have clearly demonstrated that, in contrast to the highly differentiated natural races, trout used for restocking have come from strains maintained by consanguinity over many generations in fish farming. What is more, many of these hatchery strains seem to have a common origin; since the beginning of the century, eggs of Danish origin (Nordic or Baltic sea trout) have been the strain in our hatcheries. The upshot is these young trout, fish degenerated by consanguinity, and weakened by disease, but still released just before the start of every fishing season.

BEHAVIOR

The brown trout, a territorial fish from the time of its emergence from the gravel, occupies and defends a territory that becomes ever larger with the age and, above all, the size of the fish. When adult, the fish will always have a hiding-place or a resting place

Mayfly nymph (Ecdyonum), found in running water and much loved by trout.

The appetizing pink flesh of trout comes from feeding on gammarids.

close to a hiding-place, where the current will deliver all drifting prey to its door. Being highly eclectic and opportunistic in its search for food, the brown trout feeds voraciously on everything it finds in the river, or even at the water's edge. During the first two years of their life, the troutlets consume mainly insects, crustaceans (gammarids) and other small prey (worms, alevins, water snails, leeches, etc.).

On reaching adulthood, they continue to feed on aquatic insects (larvae, nymphs and imagoes), and on terrestrial insects that fall into the water (grasshoppers, crickets, beetles, flies, etc.) and the whole of the benthic invertebrate microfauna (worms, crustaceans, water snails, leeches, etc.) living concealed in the weed beds or under stones; they will also actively pursue minnows and other small fish (gudgeons, miller's thumbs, troutlets, etc.). Halford tells how a three pound trout, caught on fly, had a compact mass of sherry spinners (very small mayflies) at the bottom of the gullet, but whose distended stomach revealed the presence

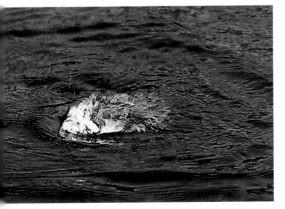

Surface swirl: the fish is feeding on newly emerged insects.

Biology

of 5 adult crayfish, the largest of which was 4 inches long (about 10 cm). Vavon cites the example of a 350 g (15 oz) trout, the stomach contents of which included the remains of 47 minnows in various stages of digestion, and another fish of the same weight whose stomach contents revealed eight large intact cockchafers, 50 or so small chafers and, lastly, an enormous hornet.

As a general rule, the diet of trout depends above all on the food that is most abundant and most readily available in the river.

REPRODUCTION

Depending on region and altitude, spawning occurs between mid-November and early January. It is often accompanied by an upstream migration of between a few hundred yards and several miles. Males and females either follow the course of the main river or enter the feeder streams in search of a suitable substrate for egg laying. As with the salmon, it is the female alone who cleans and excavates the hollow in the gravel bottom where the eggs will be laid, fertilized by the male

HATCHING STAGES OF TROUT EGGS

Egg with formed embryo.

First movement of alevin within the egg.

Rupture of egg membrane, the head appears.

Contortions increase.

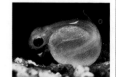

The alevin gradually frees itself.

The envelope is now situated on the side.

The alevin is free. Yolk sac clearly apparent.

The alevin hides in the stones on the bottom.

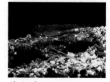

Alevin after resorption of yolk sac.

and quickly covered over. Thus buried, concealed from light and predators, they will take three months on average to hatch when the water temperature is 38–41 °F (4–5 °C).

Inside a Vibert box, showing eggs with embryos.

The alevins will remain sheltering in the spaces between the gravel and small stones forming the spawning grounds until the yolk sac has been completely resorbed. A two-pound (1-kg) trout lays about 2,000 orange colored eggs each ⅙th–⅕th of an inch (4-6 mm) in diameter. In spawning under normal conditions (size of gravel and stones, hydrology and climate), the average hatching rate of trout eggs is about 80 per cent, which is quite remarkable. While they are sheltered by the gravel, eggs containing embryos and alevins with yolk sacs are well protected and suffer only slight mortality, chiefly from predation by insect larvae. Nature arranges things very well and did not await the invention of the Vibert box for the trout to grow and multiply. Unfortunately, both for the trout and for fishermen, things start to go wrong after emergence

from the gravel. Between the time when the alevins emerge from the gravel after resorption of the yolk sac and the end of their first year of life, the mean survival rate does not

exceed 5 percent. Subsequently, as the scientists tell us, we must reckon on a survival rate of from 30 to 50 percent, year on year, up to the fifth year, with allowance for "normal" fishing pressure.

PREDATION

The bottleneck for the salmonid production of a watercourse therefore lies in the alevin-troutlet stage during the first year. While the adult trout is a formidable predator, the alevin and the troutlet are prey for a host of tiny creatures scarcely larger than

The kingfisher sometimes takes trout alevins.

Biology

CLASSIFICATION

It was in 1758, in the second edition of his work *Systema Naturae* (his great classification of species), that Carl von Linné (Linnaeus), the brilliant Swedish naturalist, classified *Salmo trutta* as the third species of the genus *Salmo*. The Atlantic salmon, *Salmo salar*, was, of course, placed first, but Linnaeus accorded second place to a "dubious" species, *Salmo eriox*, that could equally well be a salmon, or a sea trout, or lake trout. In fact, the father of modern classification and nomenclature stumbled over identification of the species *trutta* and its different forms. The Salmonidae, a family consisting of more than one hundred species, has in fact six genera:
1. *Salmo* (trout and "Atlantic salmon")
2. *Oncorhynchus* (Pacific "trout" and salmon)
3. *Salvelinus* (chars)
4. *Hucho* (Danube taimen)
5. *Brachymystax* (Siberian lenoks)
6. *Salmothymus* (Ohrid trout).

Alongside this family, we must now distinguish the Thymallidae (graylings), which are not strictly trout, any more than are the Coregonidae (European whitefish) or the Osmeridae (smelts), which were for long included. All of these fish now form distinct families within the order Salmoniformes.
Leaving aside the Atlantic salmon (*Salmo salar*), to be found on both sides of the Atlantic, there are many more species in the genus

The coloring of the livery varies greatly with the habitat occupied.

themselves, that live in, or on the edges of streams, ranging from dragonfly larvae, through minnows, miller's thumbs and eels to even their own parents, if they have remained in the stream. Their main enemy on the banks is the kingfisher; the otter, where it still exists, mainly attacks large trout. Lastly, the return and spread of two of the most fearsome predators of adult trout on some stretches of salmonid waters is to be regretted. Herons take and, above all, fatally injure many valuable breeding fish at the time of spawning in small

Large brown trout with characteristic spots.

Salmo than the brown trout — brook, lake and river trout. One feature common to all is that they originate from the Ancient World: Europe, Asia Minor, even Africa.

Thus, *Salmo trutta macrostigma*, the Mahgreb trout, was formerly common to the entire Mediterranean Basin from the Moroccan Atlas, through Algeria, Tunisia, Sicily, Sardinia, and Corsica. The renowned marbled trout, *Salmo trutta marmoratus*, used to exist in the Adriatic basin, and reached the fantastic weight of 60 pounds (27 kg) in the tributaries of the Po and in some Yugoslav rivers (Neretva). In the Black Sea region, *Salmo trutta labrax* ascended the rivers of Central Europe, Russia and Turkey to spawn. In the Caspian Basin, *Salmo trutta caspius* would also appear to have reached an impressive size and weight. Continuing eastward, into Asia, *Salmo trutta aralensis* was found in the Aral Sea, which is now shriveling away. Lastly, in Afghanistan, in the Basin of the Oxus (Amu Dariya), there is the easternmost trout, *Salmo trutta oxianus*.

The orange-flecked livery of macrostigma.

and medium-sized watercourses, and even in large ones, provided that they are fairly shallow (a feature of many rivers with large gravel beds in which trout and chars spawn). Lastly, cormorants are capable of hunting trout weighing a pound (450 g) in the deepest parts of medium-sized and large rivers, and in lakes. The efficiency of these birds is awesome, and in recent years the European char and trout populations of some of the richest watercourses, especially in eastern France and Bavaria, have been reduced almost to vanishing point.

Fishing techniques

The trout, an opportunistic predator, hunts at all depths, from surface to bottom, and can be caught by all techniques.

The trout and the largemouth bass are probably the two freshwater fish most fished for throughout the world. There are several reasons, starting with geographic considerations: introduction and acclimatization measures have had the result that it is now found all over the place, in both the Northern and Southern hemispheres, in temperate and tropical zones, provided that the water in the watercourses and high-altitude lakes is sufficiently fresh and oxygenated. Trout may be found in almost all biotopes within the same country, from small coastal streams to high-altitude torrents, in large lowland rivers and in the smallest streamlets, in natural and man-made lakes and even in managed quarries (reservoirs). Then there are cultural and historical reasons; the first fishing and angling manuals devote much space to them, but, above all, the development of fishing in general, and especially fly fishing, has been built up around this fish, to which many enthusiasts are fervently devoted.

Next there are both culinary and gastronomic reasons: although nowadays

The British technique is most effective in a mountain lake.

captured trout are increasingly given a reprieve and returned to the water (catch and release), we admit that its tasty delicate flesh has contributed greatly to the reputation of the species. Lastly, there are practical and technical reasons relating to the varied and numerous ways in which it is fished. All ways of fishing may be used for the trout: baitcasting, spinning, fly-fishing, and both natural and artificial baits.

Pierre Sempé, a master of fishing by touch, gives instruction.

FISHING TO THE BITE

This is a special kind of baitcasting, by means of which a natural bait is offered, immediately beneath the rod or at a distance, as discreetly as desired, as if it is being carried along by the current. Most of the small creatures on which trout feed in running waters are actually drifting prey borne by the current. It is the current that, in a manner of speaking, delivers worms, larvae, small crustaceans, insects, and small wounded fish to the door of the trout. In contrast to ordinary baitcasting, the leader is not supported by a float, which would be too conspicuous in clear, shallow water, and

would pointlessly slow the advance of the bait. Moreover, given that the bottom ceaselessly changes in trout rivers, the depth of advance of the bait could not be properly regulated. Fishermen have replaced the float to good advantage with simple indicators showing the position of the end of their line.

The technique was to knot three strands of wool on the line 3–6 feet (1–2 m) from the hook, but nowadays small colored polystyrene beads threaded on

---

WORM FISHING

Fishing with worm is a rather special kind of fishing by feel generally practiced early in the season, when the current is strong and the water lively. The tackle can be considerably stronger and a line of .18 to .22 mm-diameter (breaking strength 4½ –6 lb/2–3 kg) will be quite suitable. The mauvish pink worms found in the crumbling river banks are the best. They are firmer and more active than earthworms, and require either a large ordinary hook (size 6 to 8), or a Stewart mount with two size.

Fishing techniques

The fisherman should be as inconspicuous as possible where the water is so clear.

the line enable the progress of the bait to be followed along the current and down to the bottom. Fluorescent nylon line is clearly better

in this context; even when visibility is poor (reflections on a sparkling surface), visual contact may be maintained. Contrary to what the name of the technique might suggest, it is of course better not to wait to feel the bite of the trout on the bait before striking.

The trout will regurgitate should it feel the least tension; if the strike is to be effective, it must be made as soon as the line stops, or twitches, or a slight sideways movement at its point of entry into the water indicates that the trout has just taken the bait.

Tackle

Balancing and choice of leading are most important in this kind of fishing and should be quickly modifiable in response to current velocity and depth. The rods used have raised rings, and vary in length from 11½ feet (3.5 m) for stream fishing to 19½ feet (6 m) for large rivers. Some rods are telescopic: their length can be altered to suit the watercourse or the reach being investigated. The reel, needed in principle only for lengthening or shortening, can be very simple (revolving spool), but specialists increasingly prefer a small fixed spool. Use of this type of reel enables a lengthy cast to be made and the bait allowed to drift. In addi-

The left hand holding the line will feel the slightest touch.

tion, the highly sophisticated brake of modern fixed spools is a real bonus when you are playing a large trout on a very fine line.

The line should be as fine as possible, so that the pressure exerted by the current does not interfere with the drifting, which should seem as natural as possible. Depending on the state of the water, the body of the line should be between .12 mm and 16 mm (breaking strain 3–4½ lb/1.3–2 kg), while the leader should be between .10 and .12 m (breaking strain 2–4 lb/1–1.8 kg). When the water is very low, some specialists are ready to go as low as .08 mm. The hook should be in proportion to the bait used. Where maggots are permitted, the hook size will be 16 to 20. Hooks of the same size are needed for ecdyonurid larvae and large ephemerid larvae. Caddis bait (trichopteran larvae) and mealworms will need larger hooks, sizes 12 to 14.

Livebait fishing, even if using a small float, is another way of fishing to the bite that can present a minnow attached by the snout to a large simple hook or a small triple hook to large trout in rivers.

CASTING

Depending on what particular type of tackle is in use, casting is termed ultralight, light, or medium-heavy.

In summer, when the water is low and clear, light or ultralight casting is a highly sporting and effective means of presenting small unweighted natural baits (worms, insects, small minnows and such) or microlures weighing ⅟₁₆th –½th of an ounce (0.5–2 g). Modern nylon lines with diameters of .10 mm and .14 mm (2 and 3 lb/1–1.3 kg breaking strain) may be used.

Ultralight casting is precise and accurate fishing, which is especially favored in

Casting against the superb background of a lake in the Mercantour National Park (France).

Fishing techniques

A rotating spoon (size 0–1) is a basic lure in ultralight casting.

Ultralight casting: when fishing streams in gorges and wooded streams.

streams and small rivers.
In the next category, light casting has certainly been responsible over the last half a century for the catching of more trout than all other techniques put together.

Tackle

Baits of from 3 to 8 g may be used in ultralight casting. Rods are usually between 6 and 8 feet (1.8 and 2.5 m) long. When wading, a short rod, 4 to 5 feet (1.2 to 1.5 m), is preferable. The preferred lure is clearly a rotating spoon leaded on the plate, the most indispensable of which is still the cel-ebrated Mepps Aglia size 2, weighing two-fifths of an ounce (4.5 g). Some users swear by a white (actually silvered) plate, while others, whose results are as good, want only a gilded plate. In fact, the best plates will be found to be ones that have faded, become oxidized or been tarnished in the flame from a match. Devons, formerly widely used, are a little out of fashion, and have the major drawback of kinking the fine lines required here. On the other hand, small Rapala type swimming fish lures, 1½–2½ inches (4–7 cm) long, are preferable to a small fish preserved in formaldehyde, even if infe-rior to a fresh minnow. Lit-tle use is made of flexible lures for trout, which is a mistake, because models of the shad or comma type give good results. However, a fresh minnow mounted on a cap, or on a Rhodoïd disc is the best bait for the largest trout by far, espe-cially wild fish. Lastly, light casting may be used for fly-fishing where the over-arm whip action is not possible. Medium-heavy casting is used only for very large trout in large rivers of foothill (piedmont) type. The lures or baits used in this case weigh from one-half to three-quarters of an ounce (8 to 15 g) (spoons of size 3 and 4, Rapalas 2½–3½ in. [7–9 cm] long, large min-nows, small gudgeon, etc.)

BROWN TROUT *(Salmo trutta fario)*

LAKE TROUT *(SALMO TRUTTA LACUSTRIS)*

The lake trout, the lacustrine ecotype of the brown trout, certainly used to hold the weight record for a European salmonid, as specimens weighing more than 90 pounds (40 kg) could have been netted in the large Austrian alpine lakes. In Lake Léman, "whites" weighing more than 45 pounds (20 kg) were not uncommon, and only half a century ago these fish were the basis of a large commercial fishery. The main reasons why they have become scarce have been overfishing, but especially pollution, and the damming of the watercourses that feed the lakes, and up which the trout used to go to spawn. The truly phenomenal growth of these trout was due to the enormous amounts of fodder fish available in the large alpine lakes; bleak, rudd, small perch, whitefish, etc… A weight of 22 pounds (10 kg) could be achieved in four or five years of lake life. Juveniles remain two years on average in the river of their birth before becoming smolts (just like the salmon or the sea trout). The first spawning does not usually occur until after two years' grazing in the lake, after which the fish spawn every year.

In the two rivers called the Dranse in the Haute-Savoie (region of Thonon-les-Bains), the migrations of large fish were well known and were followed by local fishermen from the end of August.

The largest upstream runs occurred in September and October. As with the salmon, these fish were caught mainly with a rotating spoon or a dead fish. A few fish weighing from 11 to 27 pounds (5 to 12 kg) are still caught annually, especially since an effective fish ladder was installed (in 1998) in the Thonon dam, on the Dranse d'Abondance.

This enormous lake trout was caught by trolling in Lake Serre-Ponçon (Hautes-Alpes dept.). It is a real trophy fish, certainly as fine and coveted as a salmon.

Fishing techniques

THE MARBLED TROUT *(SALMO TRUTTA MARMORATA)*

Superb marbled trout caught on the Tarano, in Italy. This great fighter was caught on a mealworm perfectly presented by the "try and try again" technique.

fish of twice that weight were not exceptional. That explains why the few European sport fishermen who went in search of it regarded it, even at the time, as a mythical fish. The species has now disappeared almost entirely from its original distribution range because of pollution and damming, but above all on account of poaching. There are only a few Bosnian and Croatian rivers that may have relic populations. In northern Italy, in the basin of the Adige River, protection groups have been formed and have succeeded in reestablishing the marbled trout in a few stretches of the river. It was fished mainly by casting (salmon tackle), using large dead fish as bait, or lures adapted to the slashed mouth of this essentially fish-eating trout.

This trout, a native of the rivers of basins discharging into the Adriatic, was still plentiful in the watercourses of north-eastern Italy, Yugoslavia, and Albania a century ago. The *marmorata*, with its marbled brown livery, regularly reached a weight of 22 pounds (10 kg) and

Characteristic livery of the marbled trout, the gill covers of which have curious asymmetric markings.

The instant magic of daybreak, with the mist curling off as the sun rises.

not lost any of its effectiveness. The flies are intended to represent drowning insects, or hatching insects being carried along by the current. The standard wet-fly technique is to cast three-quarters downstream toward the opposite bank and to let the artificial fly or flies drift across the current. There is no need to animate

and are worked from a distance using rods 8 to 10 ft (2.5 to 3 m) long. In strong currents the lines may be as heavy as .26 mm-diameter (10 lb/4½ kg breaking strain).

FLY-FISHING

The various forms of fly-fishing now very much in fashion have benefited in recent years from considerable advances in the manufacture of rods and lines. Carbon fiber and the composites developed from it have revolutionized fly-fishing, making it easy and quick to learn, and making it a sport for many. The fact that this is an eminently sporting kind of fishing, esthetic, and even ecological (the no kill approach), was bound to make it popular with young anglers. Leaving on the one hand fishing with fly lures, or streamers (see the boxed text entitled "Reservoir Fishing" in the section on the rainbow trout), we here distinguish three basic techniques applicable to trout.

Wet fly

Although this is the oldest technique, it has

La Palaretta, a reliable wet fly imitating a trichopteran larva.

Piam, the very devil with a nymph, with one of his fine catches.

The cast must be faultless in such clear waters!

the flies in fast currents and tumultuous waters. Conversely, the left hand holding the line may profitably liven their movement in flat water and with a sluggish current. Using this technique, several flies, usually two or three, may be cast on the same leader. The leading fly will be the largest, or at least the heaviest. A classical model is selected, with wings folded on the back, or preferably with hackles of ungreased dry fly, or similar. These three flies cross the current submerged to various depths, depending on current velocity and the casting angle. The color of the various wet flies happens to be important, because the finer points of the color of these flies are clearly apparent to the trout, in a way that those of a dry fly, seen from under the water against the sun, are not. Depending on the insect food being taken, one color will be preferable to others on some days. In general, dirty yellow, brown, olive green, and black are the best body colors. In torrential or fast-flowing rivers, a touch or tap is felt by the hand holding the butt of the rod, or by a sudden pull on the line, and the fish will generally hook itself if the line is moderately taut. The same is true for very flat, slow-flowing water, where the fisherman must constantly watch the place where his flies are assumed to be. A swirl, a reflection below the surface, or a hesitation of the trace will indicate that a trout has just taken one of the flies; all of these indications call for a prompt strike.

Contrary to what might be thought, floating lines are the best for wet-fly fishing.

A perfect cast in currents.

A very bright color (fluorescent green, orange) is preferable, because a touch will often be detected by watching the end of the line. A nine-foot (2.7 m) rod or larger is needed, and it should have a progressive action, so as not to tangle the flies when casting.

In expert hands, this "rustic" technique, although far less in use these days, remains highly effective.

A good catch on the Loue (France).

Dry fly

In this case, the dry fly, preferably greased, will float on the surface and mimic a newly-hatched aquatic insect (a subimaginal stage) or, conversely, an adult insect (imago) returning to lay its eggs and die on the surface. There have been two opposing schools since the beginning of the 19th century: those who advocate a true fly copy, who try to imitate as closely as possible the insects on which the trout feeds at the surface, and the partisans of a harmonious fly, who think that the presentation is far more important than the model itself.

In reality, both sides have a point to make. Except when fishing a torrent where the trout has no time to look closely at the flies, it is important in lowland and foothill waters that the artificial fly should, on the one hand, look like the flies hatching at the time, at least in shape, opacity and color shades, and, on the other hand, that its presentation should be as good and its drifting as natural as possible. This clearly requires the angler to have at least a smattering of aquatic entomological knowledge and to be able to distinguish the four main insect groups on which trout feed at the surface. They are Ephemeroptera, the best known of which are mayflies; Trichoptera, or caddis flies, which hatch mostly at nightfall; Diptera (of the chironomid type); and terrestrial insects such as ants, beetles and

At daybreak, takes are often unobtrusive.

Fishing techniques

A cautious approach in the weed beds, where fishing is made difficult by the overgrowth.

BROWN TROUT *(Salmo trutta fario)*

Superb trout caught on a dry fly.

grasshoppers. Ever since Frederic Halford (1844–1914), published his *"Dry-Fly Fishing in Theory and Practice,"* fly tiers and makers have used all their ingenuity to establish the fullest possible collections of the various aquatic and terrestrial insects to be found at the start of the season on the river banks of a given region.

That amounts to hundreds of patterns, and one only has to look at the large compartmentalized fly boxes that many fly fisherman lug around to be convinced that the theory of the right fly still has its supporters. Twenty or so fly patterns should, in fact, be adequate for most of the situations encountered on either European or American banks. Some remarkably realistic flies have been tied using duck tail feathers, and most fly tiers now include this material in their efforts. One of the great charms of the dry fly, as of other types of fly-fishing, is clearly that the angler can make his own artificial lures.

There are hundreds of specialist books and videos on fly-tying, and it is not our intention to tackle this vast subject. Suffice it to say that making one's own flies is not too complicated, and that taking a trout with a home-made fly adds to the pleasure of the catch. As regards tackle, we have already said that carbon fiber and plastic lines have contributed much to fishing technique. Depending on the kind of watercourse (stream, medium-sized or large river), the rod is from 7 to 9 feet long (2.10–2.70 m) for lines ranging from 3x to 6x. Fairly rapid action is desirable, because it assists precise casting and penetration against the wind. As in all kinds of fly-fishing, the only purpose of the reel is to hold the spare line, and the choice should be for the lightest possible. From that point of view, automatic reels have the disadvantage of being far too heavy. In large rivers, several score yards of back-

Fishing techniques

ing behind the line will enable a fine trout to make a long initial run without any danger of the line breaking.

The length of the leader will depend on the river being fished: 6–7 feet (1.80–2.20 m) for torrents and streams, 8–13 feet (2.5–4 m) in large rivers. Also, the warier and more choosy are the trout, the longer and thinner should be the line.

Modern nylon lines are so resistant that small flies can be presented on .10 or .12 mm line. A long zig-zagged trace will, moreover, delay the appearance of dragging, the main cause for the rejection of artificial flies.

Emergent fishing

Emergent fishing, an intermediate technique between dry-fly and wet-fly fishing, and much in vogue at pre-

Trout are to be found stationed in the deepest places of this crater lake.

sent, involves the presentation in – or just below the surface layer – of models of aquatic insects (Ephemeroptera, Trichoptera, Diptera, etc.) that have reached the final stage of their metamorphosis and are freeing themselves from their exuviae. Artificial emergent flies should not be greased, but should be made from materials that maintain them in the surface layer. From that point of view, duck tail feathers are again indispensable. Moreover, their soft gray fibers perfectly imitate the water-laden, crumpled wings before they have been spread, as they emerge from the wing sacs. A swirl, rather than an obvious bite, will be the indication that an emergent has been taken in the surface layer. The back and the tail fin of the trout will sometimes break the surface, indicating that the fly has been taken.

Nymph fishing by sight

Beginning in the 1930s, and working on the principle that 80 percent of the aquatic insects taken by trout are in the larval and nymphal stages, Skues, followed by Sawyer, perfected a technique for fishing in the absence of surface activity in the chalk streams of southern England.

In contrast to the wet fly, for which the river must be randomly combed, nymph fishing by sight is a real hunt for fish already identified feeding on the bottom or in mid water. As in dry-

A standard nymph.

fly fishing, casts will be made upstream or, in large rivers, perpendicular to the current axis. Nymph fishing by sight, which is far more difficult than fishing to the take, requires excellent sight and a cautious approach to trout and grayling.

Depending on depth and current velocity, the nymphs (mostly imitations

The requirements for nymph fishing by sight are perfectly clear water... and polaroid lenses.

ing reflex in the fish. Only a very thin, long leader (at least 13 feet [4 m], with an end of at least 5 feet [1.5 m] in .08, .10 or .12 mm-diameter line) will enable the nymph to descend rapidly and be naturally presented. Dry-fly rods at least 9 feet (2.70 m) long, and with tip action, are perfectly suitable for fishing nymph by sight. In rivers where the fish cannot be seen under the water, the nymph will be fished blind. The taking of the artificial lure will be detected by a slackening, a hesitation or a lateral shift of the end of the line. A colored indicator pinched onto the thickest section of the leader, where it will function as a minifloat, will make what is happening more apparent when the water is agitated.

of aquatic larvae, but sometimes small crustaceans, gammarids) will be weighted to some degree to make them sink rapidly and drift at the level where the fish are active. Sawyer's renowned pheasant tail, a simple roll of two or three feather fibers from a pheasant's tail, weighted by several turns of fine copper wire, remains the best-known and invariably the most effective model. Made in various sizes, this type of nymph effectively imitates most of the ephemerid larvae found in chalk streams and slow-flowing lowland rivers. In large foothill rivers and other limestone (karst) watercourses which

are deeper and faster flowing, the models used should be more heavily weighted, either with a blob of tin solder close to the eye of the fly hook, or a copper bead threaded on the shank of the hook. The whole art of fishing nymph by sight is first to locate an actively feeding fish and then to offer it a nymph on a very long, thin leader, if possible precisely in its drift corridor and at the right depth. When the fisherman considers that the nymph has entered the field of view of the trout or grayling, a slight raising of the tip of the rod will slightly enliven the nymph and, if all goes well, will stimulate a seiz-

Imitation bloodworm (chironomid).

Biology

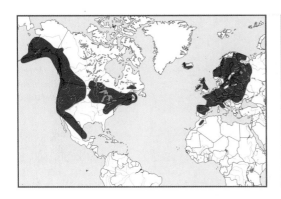

DESCRIPTION

The rainbow trout, one of the most widely reared fish in the world, has been introduced into 50 or so countries over a period of a century, and has been the subject of many scientific studies, both in the wild state, and as an acclimatized and domesticated species. This fish, which could therefore be thought to be well known, has recently changed both its name and its family. Since 1989, the International Code of Zoological Nomen-

The rainbow trout is undoubtedly the most widely reared species in the world, and France is the country with the most hatcheries.

Brightly colored male rainbow trout in spawning livery.

clature has ruled that the scientific names *Salmo gairdneri* and *Salmo irideus* are no longer valid and that henceforward the rainbow "trout" must be placed with the Pacific salmon in the genus *Oncorhynchus*, and given the specific name *Oncorhynchus mykiss*. However, the name *Salmo gairdneri*, given to it in 1836 by Richardson, in honor of Dr. Meredith Gairdner, who had largely classified the fishes of the vast Columbia Basin in western America, will no doubt appear in works of all types for many years to come. The name *Salmo irideus*, a reference to the iridescent purple band adorning the flanks of this fish, is still mentioned in many works in the French language.

The details of this change in scientific name deserve to be known. It was less than ten years ago that Soviet and American biologists

reached an agreement at an International Congress of Zoology of the International Commission on Zoological Nomenclature that the rainbow "trout" of Kamchatka and of the eastern coast of Siberia were one and the same species as their fellows in Alaska, British Columbia and California. As the Kamchatka "race" had been described in accordance with the Linnaean nomenclature, and first given the name *Salmo mykiss* by Walbaum, back in 1792, the rule of scientific precedence has to apply and the species name *mykiss* must be used henceforward. With regard to the change in the generic name from *Salmo* to *Oncorhynchus*, it is based on justified considerations of an

anatomical, genetic and physiological order. The genus *Salmo* proposed by Linnaeus in 1758 should henceforward be restricted to salmonids from river basins discharging into the Atlantic, both in America and Europe.

In the Pacific Basin of North America, between northern Mexico and Alaska, there are as many "races" and even "forms" of the rainbow trout as there are of the brown trout between Limerick and Novosibirsk. The famous steelheads (steelhead trout) stand in the same relationship to the landlocked rainbow trout as do sea trout to the *farios*: migratory forms that may

The rainbow trout is a predator that does not hesitate to attack alevins.

Biology

Characteristic livery of the male rainbow trout, with the lateral line edged in purple.

make round trips of nearly 6,700 miles (10,000 km) before returning to spawn as unfailingly as the salmon in the rivers in which they were born. Kamloops are a lacustrine rainbow trout form that may reach a weight of 50 pounds (22.7 kg) or more in the lakes of British Columbia. Rainbow trout are known to French fishermen only as the lackluster fish used for restocking, their fins eaten away by disease or by rubbing against the sides of the concrete rearing tanks, which angling societies and federations release just before the start of the season. These hatchery trout, which are always to some extent sick or carriers of various infectious agents, are degenerated, intensively reared fish that have nothing in common with those to be caught in their original environment, or even in the South of England or Bavaria. For the rainbow

trout is a magnificent fish with forms quite like those of the brown trout. Their liveries clearly differ with the race, variety or form. The livery is, in general, silvered, strewn with black spots also found on the dorsal, anal, and caudal fins. The more or less distinct iridescent purple band on the sides is the feature that gives the fish its name. As sexual maturity nears, this highly-colored band may almost completely

cover the flank of male fish. Like lake trout, the lacustrine forms (kamloops) are silvered, and have very few black spots. The migratory forms (steelheads) are ingots of pure silver on their arrival from the ocean, and it is only after some time in fresh water that the black spots and the coloration, initially pink, then completely purple, finally appear.

The head in all rainbow trout is not so massive in relation to the rest of the body, as with the brown trout. The mouth slit is also less deep.

Rainbow trout may reach a respectable 22 pounds (10 kg).

RAINBOW TROUT *(Oncorhynchus mykiss)*

Classical rainbow trout biotope in a North American river.

GEOGRAPHIC DISTRIBUTION

Migratory and landlocked rainbow trout originate from watercourses that discharge into the North Pacific between northern Mexico and Alaska on the American coast, and between northern Kamchatka and the Chinese–Russian frontier on the Asiatic coast. From the end of the 19th century, they were widely introduced throughout the world for fish farming and acclimatization. From 1870, rainbows were introduced into the eastern and central states of the United States, and then into the Great Lakes region and Canada. The first consignments reached Europe a decade or so later. Today, these trout have been acclimatized or reared in all five continents. In Africa, they can be fished in Morocco, Kenya, South Africa, Zimbabwe, Ethiopia, and even on Madagascar. In Asia, they have been introduced into India (Kashmir), Ceylon, China, Japan, and Korea. Acclimatization has been wildly successful in the South Pacific, in New Zealand and Australia. The rainbow trout may also be fished in Hawaii and New Guinea. In Central America and Latin America, they have been acclimatized in Costa Rica, Ecuador, Peru, Bolivia and, of course, in Argentina and Chile. Acclimatization has succeeded beyond all expectations in the last two countries, as in New Zealand, and many rivers of the Southern Hemisphere

Biology

today attract Americans and Europeans in search of rainbow trout.

It was probably in 1892 that the first rainbow trout reached France, not directly from the United States, but from Germany, which had been importing from America since 1880. According to Shaperclaus, three varieties of rainbow trout were interbred from the beginning and would still be the source of the "rainbows" in European fish farms — the *Shasta* variety, from California, the steelhead trout, and the *Beardsleii* variety. German, and subsequently French fish breeders wanted to use hybridization to produce hardy, fast-growing fish, able to withstand high temperatures and disease.

BEHAVIOR

The worldwide success of its acclimatization and hatchery rearing is largely due to the fact that the rainbow trout is less demanding than the brown trout as regards water temperature and oxygenation.

The knowledge that these two parameters are closely interdependent helps us to understand the successful use of the rainbow trout for

Newly hatched alevin, freed from its protective envelope. The yolk sac will enable it to survive for many days.

stocking reservoirs. Where water is not renewed and oxygenated by a current, it is necessary to find trout able to withstand temperatures of 75 to 77 °F (24 to 25 °C), at least during the summer months, and especially the low dissolved oxygen levels at these high temperatures. It is a feature of rainbow trout behavior during heatwaves that the fish swim actively in schools near the surface, rather as do sharks, to circulate as much water and, consequently, oxygen as possible through the gills.

Whereas the brown trout (except for some Mediterranean strains) becomes very apathetic and ceases feeding at temperatures above 68 °F (20 °C), the rainbow trout remains very active and continues to feed at temperatures up to 73, or

even 75 °F (23–24 °C). As regards feeding habits, the rainbow trout differs from the brown trout, which becomes a fish-eater as it grows, and is nocturnal and benthophagic (a bottom feeder), in that the rainbow trout still feeds on insects at the surface during the day, even when large. It is an enormous advantage for fishermen that the rainbow trout feeds during the day and becomes active when even a few insects hatch. As also with brown trout, juveniles feed mainly on invertebrates: worms, insect larvae, crustaceans, mollusks, etc... Adult fish are as highly eclectic as brown trout in their choice of food, and will adapt their diet to include the most abundant and readily available prey in any given biotope. Large fish are quite clearly fish eaters, but they continue, as we have said, to be interested in surface hatchings, even when the insects are minute.

In their original habitats, they breed most often in March-April and, except for the difference of dates, their spawning is very similar to that of the brown trout. Fertility, the number of eggs laid per female, is between 680 and 910 per pound (440 g) of her weight (1,500–2,000 per kg). Although France is the world's leading producer of the rainbow trout, it does not reproduce naturally there and its introduction into the natural environment must be regarded as a failure.

The rainbow trout has been intensively farmed.

Fishing techniques

Reservoir fishing arose in Great Britain and the know-how has been developed there. This highly distinctive technique now attracts many European fly-fishermen.

The rainbow trout has become a highly popular quarry with fishermen, wherever it has been introduced and acclimatized. It is perfectly at home alongside the brown trout, as is evident in thousands of rivers and lakes worldwide. The rainbow trout even has some advantages over the brown trout for anglers, and especially for fly-fisher-

The fish is on the point of giving up. It will soon be in the landing-net.

men. Its habit of feeding more at the surface makes it a fish caught, above all, on the rise; this remains true even for the largest

A ripple has been spotted. Now is the time for swift, efficient action: a cast accurate in direction and length.

fish. The fight they put up at the end of the line – at least as far as wild rainbow trout are concerned, but not the degenerated hatchery fish, is far superior to, and certainly far more spectacular than, that of a brown trout of the same weight. The rainbow trout fights in open water and in full view, away from the weed beds and obstacles on the bottom, often leaping out of the water, struggling valiantly, and interspersing its dashes for freedom with abrupt returns. Following the strike, the rush of a rainbow trout of about two

RESERVOIR FISHING

A superb trout of the kamloops strain, caught in one of the finest European reservoirs: the lac de Landie, in France.

Since reservoirs became a feature of the British landscape, fishing for rainbow trout, by far the leading fish stocked in them, has become very important. Reservoirs are radically different aquatic environments from rivers, and the fishing techniques and equipment used in them will be very different from those used in rivers. A total novice at fly-fishing will often succeed far quicker in a reservoir than will someone with several seasons' experience of fly-fishing for brown trout or grayling in running water. In a reservoir, casting is the key: lengthy, rapid casts, frequently repeated, and continued for a long time. The cast must be long, because the trout, especially those that have already been biting, are often beyond the casting reach of an average fisherman — say 45 to 60 feet (15 to 20 m). Quick casting is needed, because the fish in these large expanses of water do not have stations as they do in rivers: you will not have more than a few seconds to present your fly to a fish spotted moving at the surface or in mid-water. Casting must be frequent and sustained over a period: in the absence of surface activity in summer, because the water is too hot, and in winter and early spring, because it is too cold, it will be necessary to fish the water, tirelessly casting and recasting, methodically if

▶▶

A fine trout caught in a reservoir: When you cannot fish from the bank, a rowboat is the answer.

Fishing techniques

Two formidable reservoir fishermen: the journalists Henri Limouzin, and Marc Sourdot (behind).

possible, so as best to explore all the various depth levels.

►► In bad weather

A 10-ft (3 m) rod with 7x–8x line will be of some extra benefit in very bad weather, but our ideal is the 9-ft (2.77 m) rod with 6x–7x line for reservoir use in all four seasons, whether it be for quite unobtrusively casting a bloodworm (chironomid larva) in June to wary fish cruising around at the surface, or for presenting a muddler-minnow 65 feet (20 m) from the bank in a head wind.

Even for a single day's fishing, a fisherman wishing to be successful in a reservoir should have at least three different kinds of line: floating, sinking and intermediate, so as to be able to present flies at the various depths that the fish will occupy during the day. Standard floating, sinking, and wet tip fly lines (WF or DT) will obviously do very well, but the angler who masters double traction and uses shooting heads will have the advantage.

In fine weather

The surface water of reservoirs tends to become very hot in summer, even too hot for salmonids, which cease feeding there. Provided, however, that the lake has sufficient depth, feeding will not cease, but will merely be carried on at the lower level, in what hydrobiologists call the

hypolimnion, in contrast to the epilimnion (surface layer). The ideal means of positioning a fly near the bottom is to use an extra-fast sinking line, followed by a very short leader (no more than 3 ft [1 m]), consisting of a single strand of monofilament of .18–.25-mm diameter, depending on the size of the artificial fly. In winter, conversely, the surface layer will warm up progressively during the day, even when there is little sun, and hatching can occur, even in January. The trout will then rise into the upper layer, and the sinking line must be quickly changed to a floating line. This change in reservoir-fishing conditions is not only seasonal, but can occur during a single day, especially in autumn and spring. In the morning, before it becomes too warm, the fish will often be very active at the surface, and will subsequently move down as the sun rises, and heats the surface layer. In the evening, the opposite takes place, and in late spring and early autumn there are occasions when the whole surface of the lake may appear, in the evening, to be boiling. As in river fishing, because the sole purpose of the reel is to hold spare line, it should be simple, sturdy and light. Whatever type of simple reel you prefer, you should allow for at least 160 feet (50 m) of backing behind the leader. Automatic reels should be ruled out, because the rush of a rainbow trout of only 1½ pounds (700 g) will not leave you time to loosen the tension. There are no special requirements as regards leaders, except the use of very fine sinking line, where a very short leader will, as we have seen, keep the fly at the depth of the line. Conversely, for surface, dry-fly or nymph fishing, the leader should be as long as possible, especially in calm weather. As regards flies,

there are hundreds of articles in the fishing journals, and there have even been numerous books devoted to the subject in Great Britain, but be assured that, as in river fishing, some 20 or so models will be adequate for most situations. More than three-quarters of the reservoir trout caught in Britain are taken on streamers and attractive flies, which are the easiest to use. These flies, which are recovered by jerking movements (at the surface, in mid-water, or near the bottom), should be used, randomly or methodically, when exploring the greater part of the reservoir. Streamers are assumed to imitate a small fish, such as an alevin, or a minnow, bleak, or stickleback. Muddler-minnows and their like are highly efficient in reservoirs, but it is not proven that trout take them to be alevins. Small sizes of them also imitate the larvae of many aquatic insects quite well. Attractive flies, which are, in fact, brightly-colored

standard wet-flies, give very good results, especially on windy days. The attraction exercised by these flies comes from the jerky movement that the angler gives them at the surface, or in mid-water. As regards realistic flies, they must be even more realistic imitations of the natural prey of the trout here than in the river. In calm water the fish can take a lengthy look at what you are presenting, and at how you do it. It is here that presentation, and especially recovery and animation, are all-important.

Strike on a fish emerging at the surface; it is now hooked!

Fishing techniques

The first chironomids emerge at the surface in a colorful autumnal setting, and offer an opportunity to this specialist at reservoir fishing!

pounds (1 kg) may easily empty your reel down to the backing, and rushes of up to 200 feet (60 m) are quite usual in the large rivers and lakes in which this fish has been acclimatized.

SPINNING

Fly fishing and light casting for rainbow trout are very similar in its original biotopes to fishing for brown trout, especially in the rivers of the American West.

The same lures (small revolving spoons, Rapalas, flexible lures) and flies (dry, nymph, and wet) will be usable, and in the same ways. Natural baits also give excellent results, where their use is permitted. Contrary to what is widely held, rainbow trout are not stupid fish that leap at the first lure to come their way, or greedily snatch at a fly, however presented. Where they are fished, wild rainbow trout are as selective and difficult to deceive as wild European brown trout. For example, only very long leaders, tapering to a fine tip, and used to present small ducks' tail feathers to perfection, will overcome the wariness of rainbow trout in the Yellowstone Park. The same is also true of well-acclimatized rainbow trout that reproduce naturally in Europe, as they do in Bavaria, in Austria, and in New Zealand, where they have been successfully introduced.

RAINBOW TROUT *(Oncorhynchus mykiss)*

The little queen of North America in the net; the consecration of a reservoir fisherman!

Biology

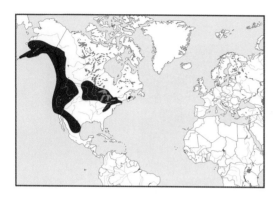

FOREIGN NAMES

*French: truite
steelhead.*

DESCRIPTION

The steelhead stands in the same relationship to the rainbow trout as does the European sea trout to the brown trout, namely it is what biologists now call a migratory form or ecotype, the life cycle of which is divided between the ocean, in which it feeds, and fresh water, where it reproduces and its juveniles grow. When steelheads return to the rivers, the head and the back are steel-blue, hence the name, and the flanks are silvered, interspersed with black crosses. As their freshwater stay lengthens, these shades darken and the iridescent purple band, a feature of rainbow trout, appears as spawning time approaches. The average weight of steelheads varies greatly from river to river, and, within the same river, by time of year or the point reached, as does that of salmon and sea trout in Europe. On the American side, the average weight increases regularly from south to north. Thus, in California, or Oregon, a fish of 10–12 pounds (4.5–5.5 kg) is

The mauve-tinted gill cover shows that this sham trout is a Pacific salmon, a rainbow trout, in this instance the steelhead strain.

One of the king fish of the reservoir, acclimatized with difficulty in Europe. The anadromous migratory strain of the rainbow trout: the renowned, and highly coveted steelhead, here proudly exhibited by Vincent Thomas, a French guide.

Biology

thought to be a good specimen, whereas further to the north, in Washington State, or in British Columbia, twice that weight is commonly reached. The record for rod and line stands at 42 pounds (19 kg) for a fish caught in southern Alaska, but fish weighing more than 50 pounds (22.7 kg) are said to have been netted or harpooned by the Indians. On the Asiatic side, especially in Kamchatka, the average weights of steelheads would seem to be roughly the same, once again with some fish reaching or exceeding 30 pounds (13.6 kg).

GEOGRAPHIC DISTRIBUTION

Wild steelheads are found from southern California to Alaska, on the American side, and from northern Kamchatka to the Sino-Russian frontier, on the Asiatic mainland.

Although there are runs in almost all the small coastal rivers, steelheads, unlike sea trout, may migrate for more than 665 miles (1,000 km) inland, in the large river basins, such as those of the Columbia and the Amur.

Following the almost universal introduction of rainbow trout, runs of "acclimatized" steelheads have been reported in New Zealand, Chile, and occasionally on the British and Irish coasts (escapees from fish farms). We should note the outstanding results from the acclimatization of steelheads in the American Great Lakes, especially Lake Michigan, a veritable inland freshwater sea, where they are one of the main sporting attractions for American fishermen, along with Pacific salmon, also recent introductions.

A freshly caught steelhead in a watercourse in British Columbia.

STEELHEAD TROUT *(Oncorhynchus mykiss)*

BEHAVIOR

Paradoxically, the mode of life of steelheads is far closer to that of Atlantic salmon than of sea trout. Young steelheads generally spend from one to four years in the rivers (two on average), before they become smolts, and rush towards the ocean, where they will also spend from one to four years (two on average), before returning to spawn. Their oceanic migrations, essentially in search of food (small marine fodder fish, crustaceans and mollusks), are as extensive as those of the salmon, and take them for several thousand miles from the mouth of their river of origin. A steelhead tagged in the Oregon was recaught by a Japanese boat in the middle of the North Pacific, more than 2,650 miles (4,000 km) from where it had been released. It may be recalled that European sea trout *(Salmo trutta trutta)* travel at sea along the shores of the English Channel, the North Sea, and the Baltic, rather than make lengthy migrations. River migrations may also be very lengthy; at the beginning of the 19th century, before the Snake River (Idaho) had been dammed, steelheads used to travel for more than 1,000 miles (1,600 km) from the ocean. The current record for freshwater runs is probably held by the gigantic Amur River, on the Sino-Russian frontier. Homing, the ability to return precisely to the river of origin, appears to be as good for steelheads as for the Atlantic salmon, or even better. Except, perhaps, for the Baltic, the trout of the European seas do not seem to be as precise in their return. The growth rate of steelheads in the marine environment is, once again, very similar to what is known for the Atlantic salmon: 6½–11 pounds (3–5 kg) after one-and-a-half to two years in the sea, 15½–22 pounds (7–10 kg) after three years in the sea. Again, as for the Atlantic salmon, we distinguish between spring and summer, and autumn and winter steelheads, depending on whether the fish, all coming to spawn together in April, entered the river ten, six or two months previously. The proportion of steelheads to survive spawning is again almost identical to that known for the salmon, roughly 10–20% of survivors, depending on the river. Lastly, like *Salmo salar*, steelheads do not feed in the rivers. If they bite at lures or flies, it is more through aggressiveness or curiosity than out of hunger. When they do swallow a cluster of salmon eggs (undoubtedly the best bait), they certainly do so in memory of past feasts, a little like the salmon taking a prawn in fresh water.

Fishing techniques

The steelhead trout, undoubtedly the fish most sought after by North American sportsmen, is a formidable adversary, whose defense is almost unequaled among other salmonids.

Fly-fishing for the steelhead in fresh water has the same regal status in the United States and Canada as does salmon fishing in Europe. Those few fishermen who have caught both species even hold the steelhead in higher esteem than the salmon, at least as regards its fighting spirit at the end of the line. The aggressiveness of the take, and the length of the first rush of a newly-hooked steelhead, are far beyond what the Atlantic salmon has to offer. The steelhead is also unquestionably far ahead when it comes to leaps and aerial acrobatics. Even very large fish of more than 20 pounds (9 kg) are capable of an aerial performance that would excite the envy of any salmon grilse newly come to the Spey.

We should, however, recognize that the high esteem in which many American fishermen hold the steelhead, compared to the Atlantic salmon, is largely due to the very light equipment used to attack these fish.

In the main it is single-handed rods and 7x–8x lines that are used. As regards the fight, the struggle of a steelhead greatly resembles that of a sea trout (*Salmo trutta trutta*) of equivalent weight. From the moment of the take, the line is snatched from the fisherman's hands and the fish, unlike a salmon, which generally stays

A sumptuous, typically North American setting, on the West coast: the kingdom of the steelhead.

where it is for a few seconds before setting off, almost invariably upstream, sets off at full speed, downstream nine times out of ten. This behavioral difference: upstream against the current for the salmon versus downstream, making use

Predominantly dark-colored flies, but with flashing patches, will stimulate the aggressiveness of the sea trout.

STEELHEAD TROUT *(Oncorhynchus mykiss)*

GOLDEN TROUT *(ONCORHYNCHUS AGUABONITA)*

The golden trout of America is certainly one of the most beautiful, and undoubtedly the most brilliantly colored, freshwater fish. It is a cousin of the rainbow trout, whose wild populations are native to the upland lakes and rivers of California above 6,800 feet (2,100 m). The species has since been successfully acclimatized in the mountain lakes of Idaho, Wyoming, and Washington State. It is the only salmonid that, when adult, retains traces of its juvenile markings on its flanks (like fingerprints) — up to ten on each side. These markings are, moreover, emphasized by the purple band extending along the lateral line.

The ground color of the body resembles molten gold, and black spots appear only on the dorsal and tail fins. The other fins are orange-red, edged in pearly white. In its original California biotopes, the species rarely weighs more than 2 pounds (just less than 1 kg), whereas in Wyoming, acclimatized fish reach double that weight. Golden trout are fished in the same way as all upland lake trout, using natural baits, lures, or flies.

The golden trout to be seen nowadays in Europe is only a pale reflection of Oncorhynchus aguabonita. Such fish are, in fact, albino rainbow trout.

Steelheads sometimes go high up rivers where the water is cool and oxygenated.

which are the most deadly bait, are fortunately banned on many American and Canadian rivers. Although sinking lines were for long used almost exclusively in fly-fishing, even in summer, the trend has been reversed during the last 20 or so years, and, even in winter, many American fishermen now use, if not a dry-fly, then at least a greased line, as is used for salmon fishing in Scotland during the summer months. As with the salmon, the choice of trout-fly — of which there are also several hundred — is unimportant. What matters is the size, its opacity, and how it is presented across

of the current's strength, for the steelhead or the sea trout, undoubtedly largely explains why the steelhead defends itself better than an Atlantic salmon of comparable weight.

American scientists even wonder whether these devilish fish, which may surface to take a dry fly when water temperature is around 37 °F (3 °C) (perhaps not the best way of fishing for them at the time), might not be endowed with a special physiological reaction, triggered when they are hooked, that could enable them to raise their body temperature to above the ambient temperature,

under the influence of the large rush of adrenaline that is a feature of the species, at least during the first moments of the fight with the angler.

All techniques used in fishing for Atlantic salmon, including prawn and worm bundles, are suitable for the steelhead. The same brightly colored revolving and wobbling lures are very successful in winter. Salmon or trout eggs,

A fine steelhead landed after a spectacular fight.

CUTTHROAT TROUT *(ONCORHYNCHUS CLARKI)*

The cutthroat trout is so called because of the blood-red mark, resembling a gash, immediately behind the gill covers. The ground color of the body is olive brown, with a profusion of interspersed small black dots from head to tail. Contrary to the belief of many fishermen, the cutthroat is not a variety of the rainbow trout, but a separate species, which also has marine migratory "forms" in the coastal rivers flowing into the Pacific from California to Alaska. The inland distribution range of this species almost exactly duplicates that of the rainbow trout. It is found in both rivers and lakes. It was lacustrine forms that reached the record weights of more than 40 pounds (18 kg) in California and Nevada. The average weight of these trout in rivers is one-and-a-half pounds (700 g), with exceptional fish reaching five to six pounds. There is little difference between fishing for them and for other trout (brown and rainbow trout), except that the cutthroat is far less wary and very easy to catch with natural bait, lures, and artificial flies. It is this fish, wrongly confused with the rainbow trout, which has given the latter the reputation of being easy to deceive. When once hooked, there is nothing exceptional about its defense, except for migratory fish newly arrived from the ocean.

the current. All techniques used in two-handed salmon fishing are quite suitable, but the use of shooting head leaders is an advantage, especially in large rivers, for those who know how to use double traction.

The hooked steelhead makes a powerful rush with the current.

Biology

DESCRIPTION

Zoologically speaking, the sea trout, *Salmo trutta trutta*, is the same fish as the brown trout *Salmo trutta fario*. In the view of scientists, the sea trout, like the lake trout, *Salmo trutta lacustris*, is merely a migratory form of the brown trout. Nevertheless, if we compare a brown trout in a Normandy river, such as the Touques, with a "white" (*blanche*) trout, which is the local name for the sea trout, it seems difficult to assert that the two fish are really genetically identical.

The two trout, which may have come from the same batch of eggs, have nothing in common. Whereas the first will weigh 14 ounces (400 g) when four years old, and will be white with red spots, which is typical of Normandy brown trout, the second will weigh 10 times as much (about 9 lb [4 kg]), and will be uniformly silvered, or have only a few black crosses. As their stay in fresh water lengthens, this livery will darken, passing from coppery to completely brown, before becoming a dead-leaf shade as spawning time approaches.

GEOGRAPHIC DISTRIBUTION

Except for the Mediterranean Basin, sea trout are to be found wherever brown trout

A large fish from the Touques river, in Normandy.

SEA TROUT *(Salmo trutta trutta)*

inhabit rivers flowing into the Atlantic, the English Channel, the North Sea, the Baltic, the White Sea, and the Barents Sea. Sea trout return, or used to return (before the rivers became degraded and the strains extinct) to almost all European countries, from Iceland, in the west, to the Kola Peninsula, in the east, and from Finland, in the north, to Portugal, in the south. Nowadays, the largest stocks are to be found in the British Isles and the Scandinavian countries. In Spain, following a sharp decline, there are good runs again in the rivers of the Asturias and the Cantabrian coast. In France, sea trout resources have been improved, partly on account of various plans initially for salmon, followed by plans for major migratory fish, undertaken from the mid-70s onwards. The sea trout, which is far more opportunistic than the salmon, has benefited from many developments, especially the fish passes provided in many river basins

BEHAVIOR
Like the Atlantic salmon, the sea trout lives out its life

in two completely different environments: the river and the ocean. Having, on average, spent the first two years of its life in the river or stream of its birth, the troutlet, previously indistinguishable from its brown trout relatives, begins to undergo "smoltification" towards the end of its second spring, i.e. to undergo a real metamorphosis that will enable it to enter salt water. In less than a week, it will discard its troutlet livery for a completely silvery coat, and simultaneously become more slender and larger-eyed.

Its behavior will also change completely. Previously sedentary and territorial, it will now become migratory and, when the moon next changes phase, the sea trout will answer the call of the ocean and depart downstream on its great adventure.

Our knowledge of how sea trout live in the saline environment is very fragmentary and far less complete than it is for the Atlantic salmon. Whereas the salmon may be capable of making the long haul across the Atlantic from East to West, sea trout would appear to move along the

coasts into which flow the rivers of their birth.

Migration and diet
During the first months of their marine life, sea trout would appear to feed mainly on invertebrates: marine worms, prawns, crabs, and small mollusks. In some rivers, fish that went down to the sea in May can return in the following August, when they will weigh between 10½–14 ounces (300–400 g). In the British Isles they are called finnocks. Others will remain in the sea throughout the summer and the following winter, and not return to the river until the end of a whole year, when they will weigh, on average, 2½–4½ pounds (1–2 kg). From a weight of about 1 lb (500 g), sea trout actively pursue schools of small sea fish: smelts, sand-eels, sprats, herring, etc.. Some sea trout strains remain in salt water for two to three years before returning to the river for the first time.

The average weight of these returning fish is around 6½ pounds (3 kg). Some fish that have spent four years in the English Channel, the Baltic, or the North Sea may weigh more

Biology

than 17½ pounds (8 kg) when first they return.

Sea trout, unlike salmon, continue to feed on their return to fresh water, although only moderately relative to their size. Their feeding activity is primarily nocturnal. Their most usual prey are insects and small fish. When the rivers are in spate, they may also feed during the day. The length of their migrations in fresh water is obviously dependent on the length of the watercourses up which they go, or to be more precise on the distance of the spawning grounds from the point at which the water ceases to be salty. The sea trout of French, Scottish, Irish and Welsh coastal rivers make only short migrations in fresh water, of an average order of 20–35 miles (30–50 km), obviously because these watercourses are short.

The record for migration would appear to be held by the sea trout of the Dunajec river, a Czech tributary of the Vistula, which runs up from the Baltic for more than 650 miles (1,000 km). The sea trout of the Rhine also certainly made very long freshwater migrations in the 18th century, to reach their spawning tributaries at the foot of the Swiss Alps, or in the heart of Germany.

Reproduction

Spawning takes place in winter, either in the river or in its small tributaries. Its features are the same as in the brown trout and the lake trout.

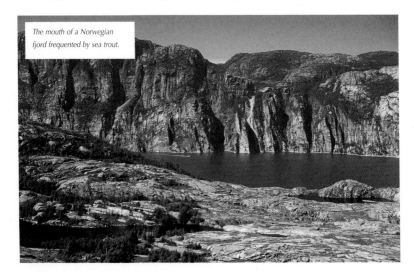

The mouth of a Norwegian fjord frequented by sea trout.

Fishing techniques

The sea trout, an anadromous migrant, tends to be crepuscular. Fishing for it is therefore most likely to be successful around dawn or at nightfall.

Grasping by the tail is a more delicate operation when dealing with a sea trout than with a salmon.

Fishing for sea trout is regarded in the British Isles and Scandinavia as being just as fine a sport as Atlantic salmon fishing. In France, it has been only during the last decade or so that this type of fishing, which is very special by virtue of its nocturnal nature, has been recognized and permitted by the authorities. Lastly, the rule for some classified "sea trout waters" permits fishing for only two hours after sunset.

FLY-FISHING
The sea trout is certainly the most lucifugous (light-shunning) of the salmonids, and although, unlike the salmon, it continues to feed in the river, its predatory activity is essentially nocturnal.

It is only when the river is in spate, in dirty water, and when the sky is overcast that there is any chance of

Fishing techniques

A superb fish caught at the close of the day on a calm pool.

making a fish bite during the day, with a juicy worm, a dead minnow, a spoon, or a Rapala. Dry-fly or wet-fly fishing yields excellent results even, and especially, when the water is very low and clear, in summer and early autumn, provided it is carried out in darkness.

In July, August, and September, it is only in the depth of night, when there is no moon, that the trout begin to hunt in the currents. Although fishing in the evening may be successful, it will never compare with fishing in the middle or end of the night, because the fish will have been disturbed during the day. From mid-September until late October, when the air temperature becomes noticeably cooler after midnight, the fish will, on the contrary, tend to be most active at the beginning of the night.

During the warm summer months and at the beginning of the night, a large dry fly, a sedge, or a palmer, dragged as close as possible to the banks, will provoke noisy and spectacular attacks.

Be on your guard against instinctively striking too quickly, and drawing a blank. Once it is really dark, go for wet-fly fishing, and fish deeper and deeper as the air temperature cools to below the water temperature. Any fly will do, so long as it is black. Vary sizes and opacity in relation to the level, the water-course, its size and the clearness of the water. In general, sizes 8–10 may be regarded as universally acceptable. The best models, or those that give the lowest failure rates, are the ones mounted on a double hook, or, better still, a triple hook of the Esmond Drury type. A tuft of squirrel, marten, or stoat tail hairs tied on the top or all round the shank of the hook will give you the best possible fly. Apart from this choice, you will be free, during your next trip to London or Edinburgh, to get a complete set of sea-trout flies, such as may be found in the Hardy catalog from the 1950s. In three sizes, and all of the same opacity, that will amount to about 1,200 flies, which will be most effectively displayed and the envy of all your friends when arranged in half a dozen Wheatley boxes.

How to fish at night

Do not improvise, if you have never fished at night. You need to have a look during the day at the places where you will fish. When evening comes, keep as far back from the banks as possible. Fish sitting down or on your knees, and cast as unobtrusively as possible. At night, even the largest sea trout take up positions in very little water at either end of submerged structures, and on the edges of the current. Should the moon's rays illuminate the river banks, avoid finding yourself silhouetted on top of the banks. The more highly raised are banks, the lower profile you should keep, and the more circumspect your movements. At times when water levels are low, in July or August, avoid walking in the water, even at the water's edge, since that would alert all trout within a radius of more than 30 feet (10 m). All actions must be circumspect. If you have to use a torch, because of tangling or to change flies, move away from the river. Should the torch beam sweep across the pool, even for a few seconds, the trout will cease biting. This fishing in the dark is exciting. When you have a bite, the roughness of the attack will take up several yards of line, and the hooked trout will almost always leap several

A standard manual fly reel.

times, before making a rush, which may be more than 160 feet (50 m) in large rivers. The mouth of sea trout newly arrived from the sea is very tender and a rough fisherman will lose many fish that come off the hook. When rushing occurs, there is no point in trying to hold a trout, even if it weighs no more than a couple of pounds. The best technique is to let the fish tire itself initially, in the middle of the pool, some way from the fisherman. Only after the third or fourth rush and the series of leaps will an attempt be made to bring the trout firmly to the landing net, while remaining ready to yield. If the night is sufficiently light, it will be better to avoid shining a light on the fish at the crucial moment of netting. The trout, panicked by the beam when the line is at its shortest and most stretched, may make a final leap while thrashing around or rushing off, and part company with you. Not until the trout is safely in the bottom of the

net can you light up the scene and admire this splendid fish, one of the finest to be caught in a river.

Fishing near an estuary, where sea trout are assembled ready to go up the river.

Biology

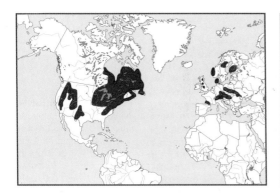

FOREIGN NAMES

*French: saumon de
fontaine.
German: Amerikan-
ischer Bachsaibling.
Italian: salmerino di
fontana.*

DESCRIPTION

The Americans call it the
brook trout, while in France
it is known as saumon de
fontaine; rarely can a fish
have been so poorly named.
Neither of the above names
indicates that *Salvelinus
fontinalis* is neither a salmon,
nor a trout, but a char, very
closely related to the Arctic
char. To add to the confusion, it is variously known
in Quebec, whence it originated, as the red trout, the
speckled trout, or the
square-tailed trout, depending on the region or the fishermen concerned. It was, of
course, the first French

*The brook trout makes
exacting demands on
water quality.*

BROOK TROUT *(Salvelinus fontinalis)*

The brook trout is a ferocious predator capable of causing losses in a water.

immigrants who gave these names to the fish, because of some resemblance in shape, and also a little in color, to the brown trout. The brook trout is certainly a very beautiful freshwater fish, and the colors of its livery are extremely rich. The back and sides are olive-green, and the belly is cream, lightly tinged with pink, and even sometimes distinctly orange. The caudal, anal, ventral, and pectoral fins are reddish, and their leading edge is double-bordered in black and white. But perhaps the most characteristic feature of the livery is the irregular pale-green vermiculation scattered over the back, along with the vermilion and blue ocelli (eye spots) on the sides. Like the Arctic char, the male assumes even brighter and more sparkling colors as spawning time approaches, and the belly,

in particular, becomes a vivid bright red. The brook trout does not grow very large or very heavy for a salmonid. Even in its original biotopes, a one pound (450 g) fish is thought good. Also, quite paradoxically, it is in the northernmost part of its distribution range, in Labrador, that the largest examples are caught. The sporting record for a fish,

that must have been more than 30 years old, caught on rod and line is 10 lb 11 oz (4.870 kg).

GEOGRAPHIC DISTRIBUTION

In contrast to other *Salvelinus* species, the distribution range of the brook trout is quite clearly delineated and restricted to the north-eastern region of North America. The western limit is in the Great Lakes region, while in the East it extends along the Appalachians to Georgia. To the North, the species colonizes lakes and rivers as far as Hudson Bay and Ungava Bay. It may be, however, noted that there have never been brook trout in Greenland.

The kingdom of the brook trout: the high mountains!

Three kings from Lake Victor, in Quebec: brook trout (on the right), also called speckled, Arctic char (center), and a landlocked salmon (the ouaniche).

From the end of the 19th century, the brook trout was successfully introduced into other regions of Canada and the United States, as well as Europe, South America (Argentina, Chile), and New Zealand. The first fish were imported into France around the 1880s, along with the first rainbow trout.

BEHAVIOR

The brook trout, or rather the brook char, is a fish of cold, pure, well-oxygenated water. Within its original range, the species develops best in water in which the temperature stays around 46.4–50 °F (8–10 °C) and scarcely exceeds 53.6 °F (12 °C) in summer.

Its diet is very similar to that of the trout.

Following resorption of the yolk sac, the young alevin first feeds mainly on zooplanktonic microcrustaceans (such as daphnia, copepods), then becomes an insectivore, feeding almost exclusively on dipterous larvae.

After it reaches adulthood, its diet becomes more eclectic: insects (such as larvae and imagoes), crustaceans, mollusks, leeches and, of course, small fish also present in cold water (chub, minnows, and juvenile salmonids, including its own alevins). In the northernmost parts of its distribution range, the reproduc-

tive period is in the autumn, whereas further south it is in the winter. The breeding fish make short migrations to the spawning grounds. As always happens among the salmonids, it is the female fish who will excavate the nest in the stones on the bottom, by abrupt movements of the body. The male stays slightly in the background and watches his competitors.

Like the trout, the female lays 450–900 or so eggs per pound of body weight (1,000–2,000 per kg), and incubation takes between 50 and 140 days, depending on the temperature of the watercourse.

Fishing techniques

The brook trout, an active carnivore, is far less wary and selective than the brown trout. Fishing for it is therefore easier and less technically demanding.

The brook trout, which is highly voracious and not very wary, is quite easy to catch. All trout-fishing techniques are suitable, from fishing by touch, using natural baits (worms, insect larvae), through spinning metallic lures or minnow and, of course, all the varieties of fly-fishing. When insects are hatching, brook trout may readily be taken by dry fly. They are therefore far less choosy than the wild trout.

One of the best techniques to use in lakes, reservoirs and large rivers when no insects are hatching, and in the absence of rises, is to use streamers, or fly-lures. The most preferred fly in the United States and Canada is certainly the muddler-minnow in all its variants (including colored ones). These models can also give excellent results in European waters.

A superb brook trout in its sparkling spawning livery, that fell to a streamer.
This fish is highly thought of in reservoirs for its magnificent colors, combativeness, and its healthy appetite.

Fishing techniques

Many Pyrenean lakes, often at altitudes above 6,500 feet (2,000 m), have been restocked with brook trout, which unfortunately fail to grow to any size, because of the scanty food supply.

The British technique is very successful in long-range fishing for brook trout in a mountain lake.

In fact, most streamers used in reservoirs, even those with the most brilliant colors, yield good results. Although brook trout are the salmonids most easy to deceive, and consequently to make bite, they defend themselves fiendishly when hooked, and put up a good fight on light tackle suited to their size. Given that their average weight rarely exceeds a pound (450 g), the strength of the rod should not be more than 4–5, and the nylon for spinning no thicker than .20 mm in diameter. Lastly, let us mention that, as with all chars, the flesh when cooked is firm, of a salmon-pink color, and very delicate.

The brook trout is also a river dweller, and can there be caught by touch, by fly or by ultralight spinning.

Biology

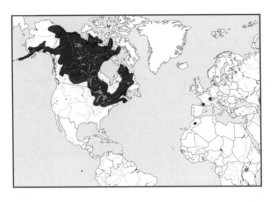

FOREIGN NAMES

Canadian: touladi, truite grise, Canadian char.
French: cristivomer.

DESCRIPTION

The name given to this fish in North America, gray or lake trout, is incorrect, because it is, in fact, a char (genus *Salvelinus*), and the giant of the family. In those European countries, where it has been introduced (France, Germany, Austria, Switzerland), the most widely-used name is cristivomer, which refers to the cristate shape of its vomer, a bone of the palate, but that name has not displaced lake trout in English. In general appearance, *Salvelinus namaycush* must be said to look like a trout. Its most distinguishing feature is the clearly forked tail, the end of which is characteristically V-shaped. Color varies appreciably with size and age, but the body is most often blue-gray, or green-gray, with more or less rounded cream spots along the sides.

GEOGRAPHIC DISTRIBUTION

Whereas the genus *Salvelinus* is holarctic in its distribution (i.e. is found in the Northern Hemisphere, in all regions bordering on or close to the Arctic Circle), the lake trout was originally uniquely represented in North America. It is certainly the salmonid least able to tolerate a saline environment. Thus, on either side of the North American continent, it is not found in Newfound-

The lake trout was introduced into Europe at the end of the 19th century.

LAKE TROUT *(Salvelinus namaycush)*

Everything about the morphology of the lake trout, especially the broadly slashed jaws, points to a ferocious predator.

land, nor on Vancouver Island, and the Bering Strait has proved to be an insuperable barrier for it.

BEHAVIOR

The lake trout is a unique salmonid in many respects. It cannot tolerate even the slightest salinity; it is almost exclusively a lake fish. The lake trout certainly holds the salmonid deep diving record: in the Great Bear Lake, in Canada, some specimens have been taken in nets submerged to a depth of 1,500 feet (460 m). Along with the huchen, it is certainly the salmonid best able to withstand very low temperatures. The surface of the lakes in which it lives is frozen over for more than nine months of the year, and sometimes almost the entire depth of the water freezes without the fish suffering. Its preferred temperature is around 46.4–48.2 °F (8–9 °C). Only immediately after the thaw is it to be

found near the surface of the lake.

As soon as the upper layers of the water begin to warm in summer, it seeks refuge in the cooler depths, where it also prefers the shade. Along with the huchen, it is also the longest-lived member of the salmonids.

Age determinations based on the otoliths (ossicles of the inner ear), a far more reliable method than dating from the scales, have established that some large fish are almost certainly more than 60 years old. Their growth rate, like that of all cold-water fish, is very slow, but that has not prevented them from reaching a record weight for salmonids, along with the huchen and the king salmon.

The largest lake trout ever to be caught by a sportsman was a fish weighing 65 pounds (29.5 kg) caught in Canada, but a fantastic specimen weighing more than 100 pounds (102 lb/46.36 kg, to be precise) was taken in a net, in Canada, in 1961.

Juveniles feed mainly on zooplankton during their first years. Subsequently, until they weigh more than a pound (450 g), they are

almost exclusively piscivores (fish-eaters), attacking all fish smaller than themselves, including their own young. As regards spawning, the lake trout is, once again, a truly distinctive salmonid, being the only species in which the female does not excavate a nest in the gravel, and bury the fertilized eggs. All that it does is expel its eggs over a pebbly bottom, in the hope that they fall into gaps between the stones, and there find shelter and protection during incubation. Spawning occurs in autumn, at depths generally between 6½ feet and 65 feet (2–20 m), but capable of reaching 325 feet (100 m) in some lakes. The onset of sexual maturity occurs from an age of 7–8 years, and the fish may spawn only once every three years in the highest latitudes.

The characteristic speckled livery of the lake trout.

Fishing techniques

The lake trout is undoubtedly the most voracious Salvelinus species. Its weight, which may reach 66 to 88 pounds (30–40 kg), makes it a wonderful fish for sport!

The main type of recreational fishing for the lake trout is by deep trolling. The lures are almost always wobbling spoons or swimming fish of the Rapala type. During the first few weeks after the thaw, it is pointless to troll at less than about 32 feet (10 m), and subsequently it is often best to deploy the lures at between 95 and 195 feet (30–60 m), rather as when fishing for the Arctic char. When the fish bites at depth, the fishing is tedious and not much sport, because the rapid ascent to the surface, with resulting decompression of the gas in the swimbladder, would appear to suffocate the fish, which does no more than throw its head from side to side a few times. However, should you be lucky enough to tempt them to bite near the surface, they make very good and brave opponents.

In France, in the Alpine and Pyrenean lakes, in which they are well acclimatized, they are fished from the bank, by spinning (mounted dead minnow, plunging swimming fish, or spoons), or by offering a live minnow

A fine brace of lake trout caught by trolling in a lake in Quebec.

THE SPLAKE

In fish farming, the lake trout may be crossed with the brook trout. The hybrid is known as a splake, a contraction of speckled trout (the American name for the brook trout), and lake trout. This hybrid, first produced in 1878, has been highly successful in North America for nearly 50 years. The splake is quite an extraordinary fish. In the first place, it is fertile, which is quite uncommon in hybrids, and able to breed with another splake, or with either of its parents. The splake reaches sexual maturity at an early age, from two to three years old, as against six or seven years old for the lake trout.

It grows very rapidly, even in cold water. In Canada, in its natural habitat, it reaches a weight of 16 pounds (7.3 kg) in its sixth year, and may live at least ten years. This fish has so much to commend it that, both in the United States and in Canada, it is regularly included in restocking operations wherever it is, or has been, present.

An average lake trout, which had to be released after the traditional souvenir photograph.

behind a sliding lead weight. All techniques using natural bait (such as small livebait, worm, caddis worm) suitable in the same lakes for Arctic char may also serve for the lake trout.

The powerful, over-developed jaws of the lake trout are clearly apparent here.

Biology

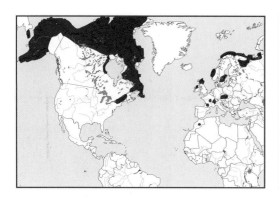

FOREIGN NAMES

French: omble chevalier.
German: Saibling, See Saibling.
Inuit: eqaluk, meaning the finest fish.
Italian: salmerino.
Scandinavian: röding.
Spanish: farra.

DESCRIPTION

In 1776, in order to differentiate the chars, Linnaeus created the genus *Salvelinus*, a Latinization of salvelin, an old name for the grayling in the British Isles. The Arctic char, which is no more than a form or special race of char adapted to lake life, is certainly one of the most beautiful freshwater fish. It is troutlike in shape, but less solid. The head, in particular, is smaller, the body more slender, and the various proportions more harmonious. In the ocean, males and females have a silvery livery, just like sea trout and salmon. On arrival in the estuary, they become

The Arctic char sometimes forsakes the depths to feed at the surface.

bluish-gray, with brighter spots on the sides: the belly is light, pinkish-white or slightly orange-tinged. As the time spent in fresh water lengthens, the back and sides take on every shade from blue to green, but, above all, the belly acquires the wonderful colors of the nuptial livery, which range from saffron

In Western Europe, the Arctic char is a typical inhabitant of the large alpine lakes.

ARCTIC CHAR *(Salvelinus alpinus)*

In North America and northern Europe, the Arctic char is an anadromous migrant, like the salmon. It is an extraordinary adversary!

yellow to the most sustained orange. At spawning time, the back may become purplish and the belly vermilion in males. There are, in fact, as many nuances and variations of these colors as there are races, regions, and individuals, and depending on the time in the life cycle. Thus, the Arctic chars of Lake Neuchâtel are generally a shade of pale yellow, hence their French name *jaunets*, whereas those of Lake Léman are pearl-gray on the back and slightly rose-pink on the belly. Other than at breeding times, it is possible to find Arctic chars that are a bright silvery shade, or somewhat darker, all the way to dark green, because the clearness of the water,

the luminosity, and the type of food largely condition the colors of the livery. The classification of the chars was for long a real headache to ichthyologists. Several tens of species were initially described in Eurasia and North America, but most specialists do now agree that there are no more than five or six true specific entities. Thus, the char of Lake Baikal, in Siberia, would appear to be no more than a subspecies of the Arctic char, just as would the char in the French and Swiss lakes. Throughout the vast Eurasian landmass, from Iceland to Japan, the genus *Salvelinus* would appear to have no more than two rep-

resentatives: *Salvelinus alpinus* and *Salvelinus malma*, which should have both sedentary and migratory forms.

GEOGRAPHIC DISTRIBUTION

The Arctic char is the freshwater fish that has both the most northerly and the fullest distribution. Its distribution range is perfectly circumpolar, i.e. it is found in all rivers, bays, estuaries, and lakes of the countries (and islands) surrounding the Pole. Arctic chars are to be found in all bodies of fresh water flowing into the icy Arctic Ocean, the Bering Sea, the Sea of Okhotsk, as well as the Beaumont Sea from Alaska to Greenland, by way of Hudson Bay,

Biology

An anadromous migratory fish caught in the Noatak river (Alaska), 125 miles (200 km) north of the Arctic Circle.

Newfoundland, and Iceland, to Japan across the vast expanses of Eurasia. The subspecies, or rather the lacustrine form that is called the *omble chevalier* in France, is confined to a few upland European lakes. In fact, as we shall see, it should be thought of as only one of the races of lacustrine chars found in France. In a great many lakes of Scandinavia, Canada, and Asia (including Lake Baikal, the largest freshwater lake in the world), there are landlocked chars that have found themselves trapped by more or less recent geological upheavals.

Staying in Europe, there are lake char populations at the present day in Iceland, Ireland, Scotland and the North of England, Sweden, Norway, and Finland, in Bavaria, Austria, and Switzerland, and in some of the lakes of northern Italy.

BEHAVIOR

The Arctic char, a boreal fish by origin, has survived only where environmental conditions are most like those found in the Arctic zone. The Arctic char, which is the most stenothermal of the salmonids (i.e. it cannot tolerate wide ranges of temperatures) can

reproduce only in water at around 39 °F (4 °C). From that point of view, the depths of the large Alpine lakes, or crater lakes, offer it constant temperatures ideal for its growth and spawning. In these lacustrine environments, Arctic char feed primarily at great depth on zooplankton, insect larvae, and small fish. In large expanses of water, such as Lake Léman, where there is a rich supply of fodder fish, lake char can reach weights of around 15 to 17½ pounds (7–8 kg), apparently a record. In most lakes in which they have been acclimatized, it is rare for their weight to exceed two pounds (900 g). In upland lakes (it should be remembered that Lake Léman is 1,300 feet [400 m] above sea level), which have scanty food resources, Arctic char rarely exceed 8½–12½ ounces (200–300 g). In the large Alpine lakes, the eggs are usually laid at depths between 195 and 260 feet (60–80 m), in areas where strong currents recreate conditions similar to those found in the river. Thus, in Léman, the char fisheries are all found on the French bank. Most of the silt load of the Rhône is

An Arctic char of a typically North American variety: the dolly varden (Salvelinus malma).

deposited on the bottom along the Swiss bank, which is clogged by it and made unsuitable for reproduction. The spawning grounds consist of small stones, ranging in size from small nuts to hens' eggs. As with most salmonids, only the female cleans and excavates the gravel, while the male mounts guard, and chases intruders away from the future nest. The eggs, which are fairly large (⅙th in./4 mm in diameter), are laid in several batches, and would appear not to be covered with material from the cleaning operation, as they are by trout or salmon. The female makes undulating movements of her body to make them slide between the gaps found among the stones or pebbles.

Net fishing in a crater lake (in the Massif central, in France), to tag fish so as to monitor the development of their populations.

Fishing techniques

There are various ways of fishing for the char, depending on place and on the behavior of the fish (sedentary or migratory). In Europe, it is mainly sought in deep water, by trolling or with a shotted line.

In the shallower lakes in which the species has been acclimatized, it can be fished in the same way as trout inhabiting the same biotopes, with natural or artificial baits. Worms, insect larvae (caddisworms), or a small live bait (minnow) on a shotted line will catch chars in the upland lakes of the Alps, the Pyrenees, or the Auvergne Mountains. Spinning from the banks is also possible in these waters; efforts should be concentrated on exploration of the deepest spots. Spoons, preferably of the wobbling kind, which fish deeper, Rapalas or, of course, a minnow mounted or attached to a Drachko, also give good results. These lures and baits are always worked as near the bottom as possible, and brought back as slowly as possible. Fly-fishing enthusiasts will find that the techniques used in reservoirs, with fast-sinking shooting-head lines, a very short leader, and black or conversely brightly colored streamers, are effective, always provided that the deep layers of the water are fished.

Fishing for large migratory Arctic char, which regularly reach weights of 10–12 pounds (4.5–5.5 kg), whether they are caught in Scandinavia, Canada, or

The winding-drum is specially designed for fishing with a shotted line.

ARCTIC CHAR *(Salvelinus alpinus)*

A fine Arctic char, caught on the bottom, in North America, using the renowned Italian "little bomber".

Kamchatka, is carried out in the same way, and using the same equipment, as for salmon.

As spawning time approaches, the males become very aggressive and attack lures of all kinds, especially if they are brightly colored. American and Canadian fishermen mainly use orange fluo spoons or Rapalas, because it is a color that seems to make the fish become highly aggressive.

The flies that give the best results seem to be fanciful streamers and models in orange or black marabou.

A completely white char from the north-western coast of the United States, caught on fly with a streamer. The fish are found to be especially aggressive near their spawning grounds.

Biology

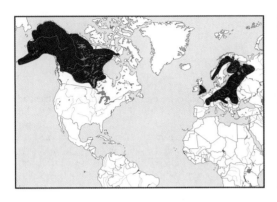

FOREIGN NAMES

*French: ombre
commun.
German: Äsche.
Italian: temolo.
Spanish: timalo.*

DESCRIPTION

The grayling may be recognized easily by its highly characteristic dorsal fin, which has few equivalents among the freshwater fishes of the temperate regions. It is huge, by comparison with the dorsal fin of other species, and looks quite like a banner. It is maintained by twenty or so fin-rays (17–25), most of which are bifid (split into two parts), to give better support for this "sail". The magnificent colors of the fin differ from one grayling strain, or even from one fish, to another. Every shade of reddish-brown and orange is present, enhanced by purple and purplish-blue shades, and spotted with black. The fact that this fin is usually larger, especially toward the rear end, in the male than in the female, makes it easy to recognize the sex of adult fish. The other fins, which lack conspicuous features, are pearly-gray, with a faint yellowish tinge.

The body is very spindle-shaped, longer than that of the trout. At the other extremity, the head has a pointed snout ending in a small mouth. Despite what may have been written on the matter, the lips of the grayling are not fragile nor do they tend to tear under the pull of the hook. They are hard, horny, and very solid. The pupil surrounded by a golden ring is another characteristic: instead of being round, it is pear-shaped, with the point turned toward the snout. Some authors consider that the rather unusual shape accounts for the excellent visual discrimination of events at the surface by this fish when at the bottom. The scales are large, quite

The grayling is still commonly called the standard-bearer, a reference to the overdevelopment of the dorsal fin.

unlike those of trout, chars, salmon, huchons, and the other salmonids. The sides are silvery, with horizontal grayish stripes, the distinctiveness of which varies from fish to fish, which are probably the source of the English name grayling. The golden reflections and gold sequins that enhance this magnificent livery in some rivers have given rise to many legends according to which the fish feeds on gold, or rubs its scales in gold-bearing sands.·

The grayling is rarely more than 1½ pounds (700 g) in weight, and around 19 inches (50 cm) in length. The largest French grayling are said to have been two fish caught in the Doubs river at Goumois, which weighed 3 lb 14½ oz (1.7kg) and 4 lb (1.8kg). In Central Europe, in Bavaria, Austria, and Yugoslavia, graying regularly exceed 4 lb 6½ oz (2kg), and some record fish reach the incredible weight of around 6 pounds (2.7kg). The European record for the grayling (*Thymallus thymallus*) would appear to be a Swedish fish caught with a spoon, which weighed 7 lb 7 oz, or around 3.35kg.

GEOGRAPHIC DISTRIBUTION

The genus *Thymallus*, as a whole, is of circumpolar distribution, i.e. it is found in almost all regions of the Northern Hemisphere on either side of the Arctic Circle, in both North America and Eurasia. The species here considered, *Thymallus thymallus*, the grayling, is uniquely European, with a distribution area at the present time extending from the British Isles (except Ireland) to the Urals.

In Central Europe, the grayling is found in Germany, Austria, Switzerland, Poland, Hungary, Czechoslovakia, Romania, the former Yugoslavia, and, of course, European Russia, including the Baltic States. In Scandinavia, the grayling

THE OTHER THYMALLIDS

The genus *Thymallus* is uniquely represented in the Northern Hemisphere by six or seven species, almost all of which are of Eurasian distribution. Apart from the grayling, *Thymallus thymallus*, the most important species is *Thymallus arcticus*, the American grayling, found in northern Siberia, the Canadian Far North territories, and Alaska. The other species (or subspecies), *T. pallas*, *T. nigrescens*, and *T. baikalensis*, are Eurasian. It should be pointed out that, contrary to what is often said, the large Scandinavian thymallids of Lapland are not *Thymallus arcticus* in the scientific sense, even if found well above the Arctic Circle, but ordinary thymallids of the species *Thymallus thymallus*.

The true *Thymallus arcticus* is found only in North America, and in Siberia, to the East of the Urals.

Grayling within the Arctic Circle taken in Lapland.

Biology

is absent from most Norwegian rivers that flow into the Atlantic. On the other hand, most Swedish and Finnish rivers have abundant stocks. The grayling is absent from the Netherlands, but present in Denmark. In Belgium and Luxembourg, it is to be found in the rivers of the Ardennes.

In Great Britain, it was originally confined to the Midlands and the North, except northern Scotland. Monks are thought to have introduced it into the chalk streams of the London Basin, and also into Wales. The grayling is highly abundant in the north of England and the south of Scotland (the Basin of the Tweed and the Tay).

Its natural southern distribution limit is in northern Greece. In Italy, it is found north of the line Venice-Menton. It has never been present in Spain, because the Pyrenees are once again an impassable barrier for freshwater species. Eastward, beyond the Urals, it is replaced by the Siberian grayling, *Thymallus arcticus pallas*, and the Pechora river appears to mark the limit of its eastern range, as it does for the Atlantic salmon. In France, apart from introduction, the grayling is naturally present in three hydrographic basins: that of the Rhine and its tributaries, the Meuse and the Moselle, that of the Rhône, and lastly that of the Loire.

BEHAVIOR

The grayling is quite clearly the typical fish of the habitat zone indicated by its French common name (see the boxed text, CLASSIFICATION, opposite). It has a liking for water that is pure, cool, but not too cold, and with a moderate flow rate (gradients of 1–8 per thousand), with gravel or pebble beds. It prefers clear water, and is very intolerant of turbidity and heavy flooding. The water temperature should not exceed 68 °F (20 °C) for too long a period. It is a species more highly sensitive than the trout to physical and chemical changes in the water that it inhabits, and consequently to all forms of pollution. It is a gregarious fish, found in schools numbering tens or hundreds strong.

Diet

The grayling is highly eclectic in its search for food, and feeds both on the bottom and, when aquatic insects are hatching, at the surface.

It specializes in the quest for small prey rarely longer than a fraction of an inch. Mayfly, caddis-fly and chironomid larvae are the basis of its diet.

In insect-rich, moderately warm waters, the grayling rarely attacks other fish. Under more rigorous climatic conditions, on the other hand, where the aquatic insect fauna is far scantier, grayling are fish-eaters, and will not hesitate to attack the alevins of other species.

The Dordogne river, near Argentat (France), one of the European high spots for grayling fishing.

GRAYLING (*Thymallus thymallus*)

Juvenile grayling, showing the finger markings on the sides.

Reproduction

The grayling spawns in the spring, after the water temperature reaches 50–53.6 °F (11–12 °C). The males, which actively police the spawning grounds, are polygamous, and may successively mate with several females. Reproduction takes place during the day, in relatively shallow parts of the river, in moderate currents, on beds of coarse sand or gravel. The reproductive rate of the female is extremely high, between 8,000–11,000 eggs per kilogram of fish (3,650–5,000 per pound), four to five times greater than that of trout or salmon.

CLASSIFICATION

Thymallus species are no longer placed in the family Salmonidae; taxonomists have created the family Thymallidae for them. The fact that this fish has an adipose dorsal fin, lives in the same waters as the trout, and is fished for, as are trout, by fly is no reason for placing it in the same family. In contrast to the salmonids proper (salmon, trout, char, huchon, etc.), all of which have a large mouth, small scales and large eggs, the grayling has a small mouth and large scales, and the female lays small eggs. The confusion is down to Linnaeus, who initially placed this fish in the genus *Salmo*, with the name *Salmo thymallus*, before making *Thymallus* the generic name. The name *Thymallus vexillifer*, meaning standard bearer, given to it by Agassiz, is still sometimes mentioned. The name *thymallus* may have been used for the first time by the Roman philosopher Aelian (Claudius Aelianus, known as *Meliglotos*, the Honey-tongued, A.D. 170–230), in a chapter on the grayling (*De thymallo pisce*) in his work On the Nature of animals. Opinions diverge on the meaning of this term, subsequently used by all authors down to Linnaeus to describe the species. It may have been derived from the fact that its flesh, when cooked, smells strongly of thyme. Other authors consider that it is the smell of the fish fresh from the water that is suggestive of the plant. According to Boisset, the French word *ombre*, shadow, applied to thymallids (*ombre, ombre commun, ombre de rivière*), was given to the fish "…because when it flees the regard of those who watch its rapid swimming, it appears to the fisherman to be more the shadow of a fish than an actual fish."

Fishing techniques

The grayling is a royal fish for fly-fishers. Although some delicate forms of fishing by touch are not to be disdained, it ought to be fished exclusively by fly.

A good catch just below a lock sill.

In England, the birthplace of fly-fishing, the grayling is not regarded as a game fish, but rather as a coarse fish, along with the roach, the chub and the dace. In the famous Hampshire chalk-streams, it is even regarded as a trash fish to be eliminated because of its competition with the trout. This discrimination is surprising, given that *Thymallus thymallus* is regarded elsewhere in Europe as a fly-fishing species the equal of the trout, and in some places (Bavaria and Austria)

as even superior to the trout. It is true that making a large Central European trout rise to a tiny fly on a very fine leader in the autumn or winter, in a large river such as the Lech, the Traun, or the Upper

Danube, is a sport for kings. Think of Charles Ritz, who frequented both the chalk-streams of Normandy and England, and the rivers of the Franche-Comté, Austria, and Bavaria, preferred grayling fishing to trout fishing, because it was more subtle. His close friend Léonce de Boisset has written some admirable pages on grayling fishing (*L'ombre poisson de sport* and *Écrit le soir*), which describe well the charm that this fish exercised on French fly-fishermen in the period between the two World Wars. Admittedly, the rivers of the Lyons region, Bugey, and the Franche-Comté could compete with the best watercourses in Central Europe at the time. The Ain river, the Doubs, and the Loue, but also the Rhône itself, at the time, and some of their tributaries which had not experienced the misfortunes of

A large grayling caught on fly.

GRAYLING *(Thymallus Thymallus)*

When water-level is low, fly-fishing is not always easy among the weed beds.

industrialization with its accompanying dams and pollution, were home to populations of grayling as dense as those of the present-day carp and other coarse fish. However, despite their abundance, these grayling were not easy to catch, and it was certainly the challenge they offered which made these fish popular in France.

It should be acknowledged here that the grayling of the British Isles, while belonging to the same European species, exhibit very different behavior from that of continental grayling. Whether it be in the peaceful and lush chalk-streams in the south of England, or in the fast-flowing Scottish rivers, the grayling across the Channel do not exhibit any of the selectivity of their continental counterparts when confronted with a fly. On Scottish rivers such as the Tweed and the Tay, it is not at all uncommon to catch grayling that have bitten at large salmon flies and even some good-sized wobbling spoons.

The grayling is regarded as a real pest in the Hampshire chalk-streams, because it does not hesitate to bite at enormous imitation may-flies that are intended for trout.

Whereas grayling more or less throughout Europe, in Poland, Czechoslovakia, Germany, Austria, Italy, and France are highly discriminating both with regard to the flies presented to them, and to the manner of presentation, the British

grayling leap at the first "feather duster" on offer, and are admittedly far less interesting for that reason.

The whole attraction of fly-fishing for the grayling, which fights as fiercely as the trout when once it is hooked, lies in the difficulty of making it take an artificial fly.

We shall see that the advent of drake-tail-feather flies has rather shifted the parameters of the problem in our favor. Nonetheless,

Fishing techniques

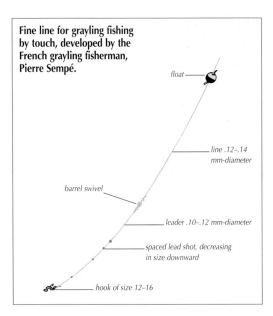

Fine line for grayling fishing by touch, developed by the French grayling fisherman, Pierre Sempé.

float

line .12–.14 mm-diameter

barrel swivel

leader .10–.12 mm-diameter

spaced lead shot, decreasing in size downward

hook of size 12–16

exactly as when baitcasting in a running river, than to make an insect larva, a small moth, or a grasshopper drift at a level. All that is needed is a small float, balanced by a line shot at intervals with pellets of decreasing size, a leader of .12–.14 mm-diameter line, and a small reel for feeding out line to a well-hooked struggling fish. Grayling specialists prefer the larvae of insects inhabiting the river as bait: mayfly and ecdyonurid larvae, caddis worms (trichopteran larvae), and even crane-fly larvae are unfailing. These larvae have the merit of being both quite plentiful in grayling waters, and of being the staple diet of the grayling. The drawback is the need to know where to find them, and getting a little wet in the process. Keeping them during a fishing trip is not too difficult, provided that they are stored in a box containing damp moss or water plants. A fisherman without much time to spare can get by with baits bought in a tackle shop. In water, colored by a spate, a small earthworm is, by far, one of the best baits for large grayling. The water bailiffs

the grayling will always remain a difficult adversary for the dry-fly fisherman, one that is selective to the nth degree.

FISHING WITH NATURAL BAITS

The grayling is as easy to catch with a small earthworm, a small insect, an ecdyonurid, a tinaeid, a mealworm, or even a maggot, as it is difficult to catch with an artificial fly. Unfortunately, the fact that many anglers fished exclusively in

this way did much to make the species scarce before limits were placed on catches. Whether it be fishing by touch or with a small float and a long drift, grayling fishing using natural baits is far less complicated than trout fishing. The reaches of large and medium-sized rivers where grayling congregate are very suited to fishing with a long flow. There is nothing easier where the gravel or pebble beds are even and the currents are steady

GRAYLING (*Thymallus thymallus*)

Evening fishing on the Dordogne (France).

on English chalk streams, who have the arduous task of destroying grayling, use no other bait than this.

Whether the fishing is by touch or else beneath a small float, the drift should at all times be along the long axis of the current stream.

Even more than with a trout, a grayling that has taken up a position on the bottom will scarcely move more than about 18 inches (50 cm) to either side of its position to intercept a prey being carried along by the current. British fishing rods between 15 feet and 18½ feet (5–6 m) long are quite suitable for grayling fishing on large gravel beds, because their great length is a help with drifting along the stream axis.

WET-FLY FISHING

This technique deserves to be rediscovered, the more so because it has fallen into disuse with the increasing success of nymph fishing for grayling by sight. The wet fly is highly effective on large gravel beds on days when there are no ripples because, in contrast to the dry fly, it may be used for the very effective "combing" of large areas of currents with a train of two or three flies. In autumn and winter, when the weather is bad, it is the only really practical technique.

Equipment

The rod, which may be the same as for dry-fly casting, should be at least 9 feet (3 m) long. The line for wet-fly casting should be floating, and only a double-tapered profile (DT 4 or 5) will enable a train of three flies to be spread out without tangling.

It is important for the color of the line to be highly visible (green or orange fluo), because the taking of one of the flies will often be detectable at the surface by watching the end section of the line. The leader should

The grayling likes broad, powerful currents on a pebble bottom.

THYMALLIDAE   **113**

Fishing techniques

be between 11 and 15 feet (3.5–4.5 m) long, with the flies mounted on short side-pieces (1½–3 in./4–8 cm).

Flies

The leading fly will often be a slightly weighted nymph or similar, with two small wet flies higher up, the choice of which will depend on the geographical region and the point in the season.

All commercially available collections of flies include wet flies, and are said to be for grayling. These are characteristically mounted on small hooks (size 14–18) and have only a few hackles.

Do not hesitate to use bright and "unnatural" colors (red, orange, pink, violet, green fluo, silver, etc.). However, grayling also readily take wet flies normally intended for trout, even on medium hooks (size 12). Soft partridge hackles which have gray and brown dots, offer a perfect imitation of the legs of aquatic larvae floundering in the surface film of the water.

Careful unhooking of a grayling taken with a dry fly; it will be returned promptly to the water.

Fishing action

This is highly classical and usually involves wading. The gravel beds are thus combed three-quarters downstream, or across very broad rivers. In the course of drifting, it is useful to reposition the line several times (mending), because the grayling does not like to see a fly being dragged, even beneath the surface. The fisherman should not lose sight of the end of the line (which is why a colored line is worthwhile),

because the touch will be detected before even the slightest jar is felt in the rod or in the hand that is holding the line.

In the summer, when the water is low and clear, the diameter of the side-pieces and the leader should not exceed .10–.14 mm. In the autumn and winter, on large rivers, .12 mm, or even .14 mm, will enable larger flies to be cast without there being any risk of tangling.

DRY-FLY FISHING

Dry flies are used in real grayling fishing. As a fish that feeds for preference on midges, sometimes all day, and especially in autumn and winter, the grayling is, in the words of its devotees, the best thing that God ever invented, and is clearly superior to the trout.

Ripples

One can spend hours, and even whole days, casting at rising grayling without getting tired. Sometimes nothing will be caught, but that

Spider.

Drake tail.

matters little, because all that is essential for a dry-fly fisherman is, whenever possible, to have a ripple at which to cast his fly. The grayling is a gregarious fish, and one that will feed actively for very long periods because it feeds on small insects. That is especially so in the autumn and winter, when males and females, which will not start spawning until late April or early May, must build up quite considerable reserves of fat which will enable them to hold out during the very cold winter months of January, February, and March.

In large grayling rivers, it is not uncommon to see uninterrupted ripples in October, November, and even December, from 11 in the morning to 5 in the afternoon. On the other hand, whereas a trout will settle back down after having refused a poorly presented fly, a grayling will continue to rise for as long as hatching continues, even if it has seen the fisherman, and even if bombarded with artificial flies. Although admittedly it will mostly not take them, it will remain actively rising, making the angler feverishly change flies one after the other, secretly hoping that each new fly will be the right one. Given that grayling tend to live in schools, there are usually several to try for within reach of the rod, without even moving. It should be noted, however, that a fly that has been refused, even when correctly presented, will rarely be taken subsequently.

The grayling will retain a memory of it for quite a few minutes, and will seldom make a mistake. Nothing is sadder for a dry-fly fisherman than a great river in which nothing is rising, and all that is to be done is to watch the water flowing by relentlessly.

Conversely, what a wonderful autumnal sight it is to see a large gravel bed with a steady current, where tens, or even hundreds, of rises produce magical round ripples that are no sooner effaced then they reappear, as if by sheer magic.

Paradoxically, when the grayling is actively feeding at the surface (when for instance, insects are hatching), it takes up position on the bottom. Should it be lying in a current of water about six feet (2 m) deep, it will regularly rise up to inspect, and to take or refuse, every time that something resembling a small insect enters into the field of its vision.

Fishing by sight among weed beds, in clear water.

Fishing techniques

This superb grayling fell to an emerger lost in the surface film.

The angler must be aware of this behavior, because it will affect how the fly is presented. Unlike the trout, which will remain just below the surface when insects are hatching and take only a few seconds to accept or refuse a fly drifting within a radius of about one foot (30 cm), the grayling will be able to detect any abnormal drift from its observation post on the bottom (especially lamentable dragging) for many seconds.

Fishing action

Depending on the depth, the fly is cast one or two yards (1–2 m) upstream from the ripple, and then drifts naturally, without dragging or erratic pauses, to at least two or three yards (2–3 m) below the fishing point. That explains the need for long leaders (at least 13 ft/4m in large rivers), ending in a very long trace of the smallest possible diameter, and sinuous casting (S or zigzagged) for drag-free drifting. Whenever possible, especially in large rivers, casting straight across, or even downstream, is highly recommended so that the fly is presented first.

On public rivers which are heavily fished, the end of the line may well have to be decreased to a diameter of .1 or even .08 mm to fool the wary fish. Care should be taken to avoid breaking the line on striking, because the grayling that has taken the fly will descend as rapidly as possible for the bottom, where it was stationed at depth. Rather than striking, it is better to tighten the line and the leader by merely raising the rod. Rods for pleasant and effective dry-fly fishing for grayling should be nine to ten feet (2.8–3 m) long when using x3 to x5 line.

There are hundreds of dry flies for grayling, but five will suffice for most situations. A small gray sailor tied with drake-tail feathers imitates all the many ephemerids of the type of *Baetis*. Another type is the small sedge, if possible also in mixed drake-tail feathers (such as the Deveux Jeck sedge). Bresson's essential *peute*, which is tied with feathers from the side of a duck, does not look like anything in the tackle supplier's cabinets, but is often just the fly needed in the water. The tricolor, also from Bresson, which imitates small ephemerids and dipterans, and even tiny coleopterans. Lastly, an imitation winged ant should be mentioned, because grayling will take nothing else during one of the infrequent hatchings of this manna. All these flies should be tied on hooks of size 16–20.

NYMPH FISHING

Although the grayling may be difficult to deceive at the surface even when feeding avidly, it is easy to take with a nymph when it is feeding on the larvae of aquatic insects on the bottom or in mid water. It is so effective that some fishing societies, confronted by the abuses of some rather unscrupulous nymph-fishermen, have banned the technique. The grayling on the bottom, unperturbed by the presence of the fisherman on the bank, will take a well-presented small nymph drifting at a proper height in its drift corridor, sometimes almost beneath the rod. The most important thing, as with the trout, is to spot an active fish on a gravel bed or in a corridor between weed beds. A very long leader (about 4–5 yards/4–5 m), ending in a long, thin trace (at least one yard [1 m] of .08 or .1 mm line) will enable the small weighted nymph to descend rapidly to the depth of the fish. When the fisherman thinks that his imitation has entered the field of vision of the fish (some experts are able to follow their nymph by sight), slightly raising the tip of the rod will enliven the nymph, which will generally be taken when moving. The amount of weighting used will depend on depth and current velocity. In rivers of the chalk-stream type, Sawyer's pheasant tails, lightly weighted with fine copper wire, can be presented at depths down to two feet (60 cm). In faster and deeper rivers, nymphs weighted more heavily, with a copper bead or a small blob of solder, are preferable. Sawyer's renowned bug and Guy Plas' Bibi, which are imitation caddis worms, are the most successful examples. It has also been noted that the grayling is attracted on occasion from quite a distance by a hint of golden tinsel, and that colored bodies (green, yellow, or fluorescent orange) do not disturb it, quite the opposite. Lastly, as in trout fishing, it is possible to fish the water without having spotted any fish, by pinching an indicator on the end of the line, or preferably at the start of the leader. Although this technique is quite effective in large rivers in which the fish cannot be seen from the bank, it is, in our opinion, closer to baitcasting than to real fly-fishing.

The difficult choice of fly.

Biology

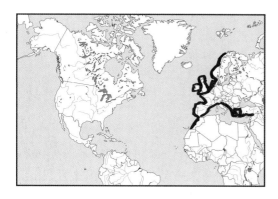

DESCRIPTION

A freshly caught allis shad is a splendid fish whose scales flash in the sun. The back is blue-green with iridescent violet bands, the sides are lighter with metallic luster, and the belly is a fine pearly white. A large black spot, clearly apparent behind the gill-cover, is all that remains of the many black marks spaced out along the curve of the back in young fish. The eye is quite distinctive, vertically obscured by a kind of double eyelid. Usual lengths are from 16 inches to 2 feet (40–60 cm) for a weight of from 2 to 6½ pounds (1–3 kg). Males are generally smaller than females. The body is clearly laterally flattened and has large, very thin, and regularly spaced scales. It is a feature of these fish, one that they share with most clupeids, that they have a saw-toothed carena under the belly, in front of the anal fin. The mouth is of medium size, but the protractile lower lip may be formed into a funnel to gather plankton. The distinctly forked tail fin is indicative of a good swimmer capable of facing the strongest river currents.

The allis shad, also called allice shad, or just shad, belongs to the family Clupeidae, in which the more

The allis shad is coming back in some numbers to French rivers.

than 170 species listed are grouped into at least 50 genera. Most species are marine fish, best known of which are herrings, sprats, and sardines. The clupeids include species from cold waters – such as herring, from temperate waters – such as sardines, and from warm waters – such as *Sardinella*. They are planktophages (plankton-feeders), which have gill arches of very fine lamellae, known as branchiostegal rays, that serve to filter the water and retain the plankton components. Clupeids, which usually form vast schools, are heavily exploited by commercial fishermen.

The genus *Alosa*, whose life cycle is lived out partly in fresh water and partly in salt water, is noteworthy for the external similarity of its members. Two species and one subspecies are distinguished in Europe: *Alosa alosa*, already mentioned, *Alosa fallax*, the twaite shad, and *Alosa fallax nilotica*, the shad of both the Rhône and the Nile, now recognized as one and the same species. In North America, *Alosa sapidissima*, the American shad, a species very close to the allis shad and also

Allis shad trapped in a drift net.

known as the "poor man's salmon", enters the coastal watercourses from northern Florida to Quebec. This species was successfully introduced at around the end of the 19th century on the Pacific seaboard, from California to Alaska.

GEOGRAPHIC DISTRIBUTION

The allis shad is found on European coasts from the Arctic Circle (north of Norway) to the Strait of Gibraltar in the south.

Shad also go up some Moroccan watercourses discharging into the Atlantic. Only a few estuaries are entered in the British Isles and Ireland. The rivers most frequented in the past

were large rivers discharging into the English Channel and the Atlantic: Seine, Loire, Garonne, and Adour. Large numbers of shad also used to enter the Elbe and the Rhine. Like salmon, shad used to travel more than 600 miles (1,000 km) up the Rhine, and there were some spawning grounds near Basel, in Switzerland.

Although the species most represented in the Mediterranean are the twaite shad and the Egyptian shad, the allis shad used to go up the Rhône as far as Switzerland, and the Saône to well beyond Mâcon. Nowadays it has almost disappeared from this basin, mainly on account of hydraulic engi-

Biology

neering works. Although shad are excellent swimmers, they cannot leap nearly as well as salmon, and the smallest threshold defeats and exhausts them. When they come up against a dam or weir that does not have a fish ladder, their fate is unfortunately sealed, even if the difference of elevation is very small.

A few fish do succeed in getting through the locks with the canal boats in the large navigable rivers, but still not enough for large-scale reproduction.

In the Rhône, the last allis shad appear to spawn mainly in the Gardon, and in the return channel of the river. The shad disappeared from the Seine around 1925, when hydraulic engineering works were carried out for navigational purposes. In the Loire, the runs are clearly declining, but around 20–40 tons of this fish are still taken annually by nets stretched across the river.

BEHAVIOR

The allis shad is, like the salmon, an anadromous fish, which spends the greater part of its life in the sea and enters fresh water to spawn. Whereas shad may travel as far up rivers as the salmon, their marine migrations do not appear to take them beyond the continental shelf. We actually know very little about their marine phase.

Migration

As with most marine

The allis shad goes up the rivers in May to reproduce.

species, migration appears to be influenced, if not determined, by surface temperatures. When shad are caught in the sea, the water temperature is always between 55 and 66 °F (13–19 °C). Tagging experiments have never yielded significant results, because shad react very badly to the stress involved. Moreover, because they are of lesser economic impor-

tance than salmon and other species, it has to be admitted that their marine life has hitherto been of little interest to commercial fishery scientists. Like most plankton-feeders, shad feed mainly in the upper layers of the ocean.

There they find an abundance of marine zooplankton: microcrustaceans, copepods, crab larvae, prawns, alevins of other species, and cuttlefish and squid larvae. Nonetheless, fishing boats have caught them in winter on the edges of the continental shelf, where depths are from around 490 to 650 feet (150–200 m). Male shad spend on average three to four years in the sea before returning to spawn, and rarely weigh much above three pounds (1.5 kg). Females remain for four to seven years in the sea, and have a maximum weight of about nine to ten pounds (4–4.5 kg) when they enter the estuaries. Shad cease feeding in fresh water. As they swim upstream they use up the fat reserves accumulated during their sea life. Because their flesh deterio-

Engineering works (weirs and other barriers) include fish ladders to enable shad to return.

rates rapidly, it is only at the beginning of the run that it is worth the while of commercial fishermen to seek them. Unlike salmon, which may remain in the estuaries almost throughout the year, and which generally advance slowly toward their spawning grounds, almost all the shad enter fresh water at the same time and move rapidly upstream. Water temperature in the estuaries has to be above 54 °F (12 °C) for the migration to start. Conse-

quently, shad in the more southern latitudes enter the estuaries somewhat earlier in the season.

The heaviest runs occur in April and May. In southwestern France the shad is definitely the fish of choice for Easter and First Communion meals.

A classical nymph for shad.

Reproduction

Spawning, which usually takes place in June, when water temperature reaches around 63–65 °F (17–18 °C), is spectacular and covers a radius of several hundred yards (meters). As it becomes dark, the fish congregate in large numbers in the spawning ground, located where the current is strongest in the middle of the river, and they almost invariably start turning anticlockwise. As it gets

Biology

Lamprey and shad are the victims of estuary fishermen using nets and traps. Even so, reasonable catches of this type could be considered, provided that there are sufficient migrating fish.

darker, males and females rise to the surface, and just before midnight eggs and sperm are emitted into the water in a great aquatic tumult. On the banks of the Garonne, this display is known as the *bull*, meaning a hubbub, and people who live along the banks will tell you that when the shad are plentiful it is impossible to sleep with the windows open. The purpose of this hullabaloo at the surface is to stir up the water for good contact between eggs and spermatozoa.

Large females may lay 200,000 to 500,000 eggs, each 0.039 in. (1 mm) in diameter, in five or six batches. Once fertilized, they take up water and swell, and sink to the bottom, where they slip between the stones and coarse gravel. The nature of this bottom substrate is very important. The extrac-

tion of aggregates from the river beds is second in importance only to the dams and weirs that prevent the shad from migrating upstream as a cause of the disappearance of shad. In water at a temperature of 65–66 °F (18–19 °C), the eggs hatch very rapidly, after four days, and resorption of the yolk sac takes the same time.

The alevins feed voraciously, initially on phytoplankton and then on zoo-plankton, soon graduating to insect larvae (Ephemeroptera, Trichoptera, and Diptera).

Bloodworms, chironomid larvae, are a favorite food. The small shad, which reach a length of 2½–3 inches (7–10 cm) by the end of the summer, even take drifting insects on the surface. The move toward brackish estuarine waters begins before the end of the autumn.

Nearly 90 percent of shad die after spawning, and it is unusual to catch fish that have already spawned. Further north in colder water, repeat spawnings of allis shad are reported. It is a feature of this fish that it is very delicate and sensitive to stress. Consequently there is no justification for a no-kill policy in shad fishing, because a fish, even when released where the prevailing conditions are good, does not usually survive the stress of having been caught.

A net stretched across an estuary is a deadly trap for anadromous migrants!

Fishing techniques

Still called "the poor man's salmon," the allis shad is a hard adversary against which to pit oneself near all its spawning grounds, usually downstream from uncrossable stretches.

Ever since the Middle Ages, allis shads have been intensively fished in the rivers of all European countries into which they have entered. They have been fished with gill nets, drift nets, trammels, seines, square dipping-nets and spoon nets (ingenious systems of giant revolving dip-nets fastened to the bank). Shad fishing as a sport has, however, been a recent development. Until the beginning *Dull nymph for shad.* of the 1970s, for as long as the returns of Atlantic salmon to the same rivers were at least average, if not good, it was toward the salmon that rod fishermen directed their main efforts. The catching of allis shad, the "poor man's salmon", was left to commercial fishermen. Paradoxically, the very costly programs for the construction of fish ladders, primarily intended for salmon, have benefited the shad above all, and shad stocks have recovered quite remarkably since the early 1980s, as in the Garonne and the Dordogne. At the same time, sport fishermen found that although shad did not feed in fresh water, they did bite very well at small metal lures, or small brilliant colored flies: furthermore, they found that, when fairly light tackle was in use, shad put up a diverting and highly acrobatic defense. It should, however, be noted that these fish are aggressive, ready to bite, and combative mainly during the first few weeks only following their arrival in fresh water.

CASTING

Shad are interested only in quite small shiny lures, such as small revolving spoons, micro-wobblers, or spoon-flies. As the pools in which they take up stations and congregate are usually downstream from dams

Rotating spoon for shad fishing, with a buck-shot pellet as a weight.

The plain hook is better at penetrating the horny jaws.

and weirs in large rivers, quite heavy weighting some distance back on the line, or on a loop, is needed for these small lures for them to be cast with a fairly long rod (9 – 10 ½ f t / 2.80–3.20 m). A thin line, no more than .22 mm in diameter or, better still, fine braided polyethylene (.12–.16 mm), for good striking at some distance, will enable long casts to be made.

brilliantly colored fly-lures, which the fisherman will animate by slight wrist movements, as they drift downstream, exactly as when fishing for sea trout. Streamers imitating alevins are quite suitable. In the United States, in many of the coastal streams along the east and west coasts, shad are much fished for by recreational fishermen, usually by fly.

A fantasy streamer.

FLY-FISHING

Many fly-fishermen use 14 foot or 15 foot (4.3 or 4.6 m) salmon rods to cope with the casting conditions in large rivers. Unfortunately, we have to admit that there is not much sport in the fight put up by a shad of the average weight of 3 or 4 pounds (1.35–1.8 kg) when such material is used. Good casters find an excellent compromise in the material used for long-distance casting in reservoirs (a 10 ft/3 m rod, with x6–x7 line). The line should be floating, or preferably intermediate, when presenting a train of two or three small

NYMPHS AND STREAMERS

Variously highly-colored nymphs and streamers taken by the shad.

Biology

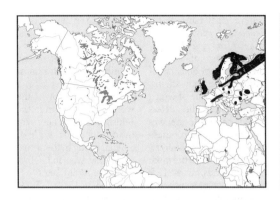

FOREIGN NAMES

French: lavaret.
German: Renke,
Maräne.
Spanish: timalo.

The powan (also known as pollan, European whitefish) really looks like a whitefish, with its body covered in large silver scales. However, this species lives only in the very cold waters of upland lakes.

DESCRIPTION

The *Coregonus* species, for long classified within the family Salmonidae, are in fact close in appearance to whitefishes in the American sense. The fact that they have an adipose fin and a preference for cool waters, like the grayling, led the first systematists to include them in the trout and salmon family. Nowadays, they form a separate family, the Coregonidae. Despite this clarification, the matter is not simple. There are currently few fish that so divide ichthyologists as regards their origin, evolution, geographic distribution, and classification. The most cautious find it convenient, at least in Europe, to speak of the *"Coregonus lavaretus* complex" when describing the various species; this is a grouping that can accommodate the fish that are native to a few lakes in the British Isles, the periphery of the Baltic, and the large French, Swiss, Italian, German and Austrian Alpine lakes. Things would appear to be even more complicated in France, on account of the many introductions and restockings over more than a century. If we

believe Spellman in his *Faune des poissons d'eau douce de France*, 1961 (Freshwater Fishes of France): "Repeated introductions of various coregonid strains, the precise nature of which cannot often be determined, has made the present populations of these lakes (Léman, le Bourget, Annecy, Aiguebelette) more or less hybrids, whose lack of homogeneity is such that it is impossible to identify them precisely."

What is, however, admitted by all scientists is that all coregonids were originally marine fish, whose growth took place in the ocean and which went up rivers to lay their eggs. Numerous coregonid species living in Alaska, Siberia, and on the periphery of the Baltic and the White Sea still follow this ancestral, migratory existence, dividing their time between fresh water and salt water. It was the great geological upheavals of the Ice Ages that confined the coregonids to Alpine lakes in mainland Europe, and to a few lakes in the British Isles. The isolation of these populations would subsequently have resulted in the appearance of many subspecies.

THE SUBSPECIES
Coregonus lavaretus

This species (including many subspecies and hybrids) is the one most widely distributed in Europe and probably in the world. It is found from the British Isles to the northernmost parts of the whole of Siberia, taking in the whole of Scandinavia and, obviously, the Alpine lakes.

The powan (pollan, European whitefish) is a "small" coregonid, rarely more than 16 inches (40 cm) long. Within its Holarctic range, especially in the north of Scandinavia and in Russia, it may reach weights of about four pounds (2 kg).

In France, it would appear that the powan existed in two lakes before there was any restocking (le Bourget and Aiguebelette). The powan of the lake at Annecy came from restocking operations from the middle of the 19th century onwards with fish from Lake Constance, and subsequently from le Bourget. In Germany, the purest individuals are still to be found in Lake Constance. The lacustrine species is essentially a plankton-feeder, but it also consumes insect larvae and, in the case of very

Biology

large fish, alevins. Reproduction is in November to December. The subspecies found in the le Bourget lake spawns on the stony banks at very slight depths.

The females, which are very prolific, lay between 11,400 and 13,600 eggs per pound of body weight (25,000–30,000 per kg).

Coregnous fera

C. fera, still known locally in Lake Léman (Lake Geneva to the Swiss), as *pallée du Léman*, is a large coregonid, which may there reach a length of two feet (60 cm) and a weight of about five pounds (2.2 kg). Apart from its size, it is distinguished from the powan by the fact that its gill arches have relatively few (20–34), short branchioste-gal rays, whereas those of the powan are longer and more numerous (31–44). The present-day Léman population could have come from millions of alevins imported from Lake Neuchâtel by the Swiss from the year 1923 onward. The old forms present in Lake Léman, also known as *gravenches*, seem now to have been absorbed by hybridization. *C. fera* lives deep in the lake, but rises up with the vertical migrations of the plankton. Small crustaceans, mollusks, and insect larvae are a large part of the diet, along with alevins of other species for the largest fish. Spawning is later than for the powan, at the end of December, and the eggs are laid on patches of small stones at depths of as much as 65 feet (20 m). A two-pound (1 kg) female lays about 30,000 eggs one hundredth of an inch (2.5 mm) in diameter.

Coregonus albula

This fish, known as the whitefish to the British, is present in a few lakes left over from the Ice Ages in Britain and Ireland, and all along the periphery of the Baltic. In France, where it is known as *petite marène*, this species is confined to Lake Chauvet (Massif central), where it was probably introduced during the 19th century. A plankton-feeder, like most other lacustrine coregonids, it rarely reaches a length of one foot (30 cm).

Lastly, the existence of several other coregonid species in northern Europe should be noted: *Coregonus oxyrhinchus*, in particular, which has retained its migratory habits all along the periphery of Scandinavia.

The powan likes rocky beds, and may remain at a depth of several meters.

Fishing techniques

Except for commercial fishing for the powan with nets and traps, almost the only method of fishing is vertical dangling using very small lures.

Powan fishing at great depth in an Alpine lake, immediately beneath the rod.

More or less wherever coregonids are to be found in rivers (Scandinavia, Russia, Canada, United States), they bite well when lures imitating small prey, especially flies, are presented.

It is usually when wet-fly-fishing for grayling or trout, above all with small weighted nymphs, that there is a surprise catch of a mountain whitefish, which is the American name. Coregonids defend themselves well in a strong current, quite as well as would a grayling of the same weight.

DANGLING

Fishing for these fish with rod and line in the large Alpine lakes is conducted in a somewhat original way in France, and also in Bavaria and Switzerland, by what is known as sounding, in small boats. It is a variant of long-lining used to present imitations of the usual prey of the powan at different depths. As there is no question of imitating small zooplankton organisms, flies are used to imitate insect larvae, especially chironomids. A fiberglass rod, or preferably a carbon fiber rod, is used to dangle a weighted train of flies at depth, using a heavy lead weight (one-third to one ounce/10–30 g) chosen in relation to the depth of the lake and possibly to current strength. As with long-lin-

Fishing techniques

The train of imitation flies is slowly animated, at the bottom or in mid water, in vertical dangling.

ing, the actual fishing technique is to let the weight touch the bottom vertically beneath the boat, and then to dangle the flies in the same way as chironomid larvae would sway when seeking to reach the surface. The touch of coregonids is so light that only a highly sensitive line (.14–.16-mm diameter for the body of the line) will let it be felt when the depth is more than 65 feet (20 m). The side pieces (of the same diameter as the body of the line) holding the flies will be short (1–2 in./3–5 cm), to minimize the risk

of tangling. It is probably unnecessary to point out here that when a pollan weighing more than about two pounds (1 kg) has been hooked at a depth of 65 feet (20 m), a very well-regulated ratchet will be needed to bring it up without breaking to within reach of the landing net. Some specialists prefer to use a frame that leaves the rod, put down on the bottom of the boat, lighter and more sensi-

tive. The number of flies permitted may vary from lake to lake, and depending on local regulations.

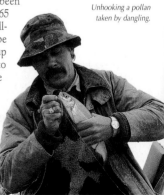

Unhooking a pollan taken by dangling.

THE INCONNU, OR SHEE-FISH

Stenodus leucichthys is undoubtedly a coregonid, but the giant of the family, because the record weight for a fish caught in Alaska by rod and line is just under 54 pounds (24.4 kg), and fish of nearly twice that weight are said to have been netted or speared by the Inuit in the icy expanses of Hudson Bay or in the far north of Siberia. This coregonid could undoubtedly not reach such weights by feeding solely on plankton and insect larvae, like most other members of the family. The shee-fish (from the Eskimo Chi fish) is a fish-eating predator that feeds in the ocean on schools of capelin and other oily fodder fish. The first French trappers in the Canadian Far North called it the *inconnu*, meaning unknown, because the species had not been classified by scientists at the time. Its distribution range is completely circumpolar, because it is found on the Eurasian side from the shores of the White Sea to the Bering Strait, and on the American continent from Alaska to Baffin Land. It should be noted that it is present in the large lakes of north-western Canada (Great Bear Lake and Great Slave Lake) and in the Caspian Sea, where it is becoming extinct. With the exception of the landlocked populations, the inconnu is a great migratory voyager, which will readily travel more than 650 miles (1,000 km) to reproduce. Those few fishermen who have been able to join battle with it, regard it as a fantastic sport fish for its valiant fight, like salmon and chars. The many leaps that it makes when hooked, in an attempt to rid itself of the hook, have earned it the title of the tarpon of the Far North. It is fished with lures imitating small fish (such as lures, Rapalas, and flexible lures), or with flies with streamers.

A superb shee-fish from the Kobuk river, in Alaska, caught by spinning near its spawning grounds.

PREDATORY
COARSE FISH

Biology

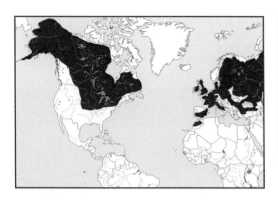

FOREIGN NAMES

French: brochet.
German: Hecht.
Spanish: lucio.
Italian: luccio.

DESCRIPTION

The northern pike is also called in French *bec-de-canard*, meaning duck-billed. This curious nickname is used by anglers to refer to the highly distinctive morphology of the snout of this predator, which is a formidable grasping tool, armed with some 700 needle-sharp teeth ranged on the jaw arches, but also on the tongue and the roof of the mouth. The picture created is as follows: Master Pike is exclusively a carnivore, one capable of exhibiting astonishing opportunism in his choice of prey — fish under the water, but also amphibians, young birds, and snakes on the surface, and so on, and sometimes just a plump wriggling earthworm.

The pike is one of the most deadly aquatic predators, one that mainly ambushes its prey, to which end nature has endowed it with the most sophisticated means.

Its upper and lower jaws have many small pores, which play an essential part in its static-acoustic functioning, and perception of

The pike has sophisticated cephalic pores, receptors that provide it with information on its environment.

The pike merges perfectly with its background.

the smallest vibrations. These cephalic pores are connected with the sense organs of the lateral line through the bones and provide the pike with information on all that happens in its immediate vicinity. Its prey must be extremely wary to escape from its unavoidable "radar beam".

The colors of its livery also show it to be an ambushing predator: with its bronze-green back and flanks shot with yellowish reflections, the pike is perfectly mimetic in the underwater vegetation of its environment, in which it is well hidden.

GEOGRAPHIC DISTRIBUTION

This superb predator, present throughout northern Europe, but also found in western Europe, as far as Spain, and in Morocco, where it was introduced during the colonial period, is also found in a large part of North America.

BEHAVIOR

Despite its seeming invulnerability, this predator is sensitive to attacks on its reproductive capacity. Water plants just below the

surface, in calm water, are essential as supports for the attachment of its eggs, and for the survival of its alevins at the start of their existence. In rivers, for example, the pike often takes advantage of a flood to venture into the inundated meadows, and there lay its eggs. Unfortunately, the straightening of watercourses, and flood-prevention measures, have the effect of denying the fish access to their preferred spawning grounds. Likewise, eggs laid in a reser-

The pike always attacks its prey on the beam, so as to swallow it head first.

Biology

THE MUSKELLUNGE, A FORMIDABLE PREDATOR (ESOX MASQUINONGY)

The muskellunge, a fish of large lakes of the northeastern United States, is a species of calm water and rich vegetation. It is recognizable by its slender body, which is more spindle-shaped than that of its close relative, the northern pike. It also has a different livery, including black bands and patches on its flanks. Its growth rate is exceptional. It may reach a length of 1 foot (30 cm) in a month, and an adult fish may reach nearly 6 feet long (1.80 m). Even so, a muskellunge does not generally exceed a weight of 65 pounds (30 kg), although records of 100–110 pounds (45–50 kg) may already have been recorded. Some specialists consider that this ferocious predator, which hunts at all depths, and frequently at the surface, would eliminate all animal life (ducklings, aquatic rodents) from a water wherever it is very abundant. According to the French journalist, Pierre Affre, this pike got its name from the word masquallongé, in the old French spoken in Quebec meaning "having an elongated masque", a reference to the flattened duck-billed muzzle of the fish. Other authors find the origin of the name in the corruption of two words in the dialect of the Cree: mas, meaning horrible, or ugly, and kinenge, meaning fish. Pierre Affre, who finds the shape slender and rather splendid, prefers the first explanation, which reminds him that French was the first language spoken on the banks of the North American Great Lakes: Erie, Huron, and Michigan.

voir lake often come to harm in abrupt water releases.

The best rates of reproduction are found in natural lakes, and especially in ponds. When water temperature reaches 50 °F (10 °C), the fish congregate in small troops. The female lays her eggs in small batches, which are fertilized by any number of different males.

The genetic mixing resulting from this polyandry is excellent for the future of the species. Each spawning female lays about 9,000 eggs per pound of body weight (20,000 per kg), which take about 10 days to incubate. The alevins then remain passive for a further 10 days, until the yolk sac has been completely resorbed. After that they disperse, to feed on plankton, before becoming true predators.

One tidbit: The female, generally far larger than the accompanying males, will not hesitate to add one of her courtiers to her food for the day, once spawning is over! In this, she is just like the pikelets, which enthusiastically give themselves over to cannibalism!

Spinning for pike, near a reed-bed, in an Irish lough, in County Cavan.

THE OTHER AMERICAN PIKE

Redfin pickerel *(Esox americanus americanus)*
This pike, scarcely exceeding 2½ pounds (1 kg), is easily recognizable by its brick-red fins. It is found mainly in the lakes and calm rivers in the east of North America.

Grass pickerel *(Esox americanus vermiculatus)*
This pike, of the same average size as the redfin pickerel, differs in having duller, greenish to dark-brown fins. Its flanks have transverse bronze bars.

Chain pickerel *(Esox niger)*
As its name indicates, this pike has a duller livery than its two homologs. The flanks are decorated with yellowish areas of variable size, edged by wavy bronze-to-blackish lines linked to form a chain pattern. The maximum weight is about 9 pounds (4 kg).

Despite their reduced average size, these three American pike are highly thought of by anglers, for their combativeness, and other qualities. They should be fished using light tackle, in order to enjoy the fight they put up!

Biology

PROFESSIONAL SECRETS

RAYMONDO THE GUIDE, KNOWN AS RAY

Everyone around Maquinenza, in Spain, knows Ray, a recognized specialist on record catfish and pike. He tracks down Master Pike in the ox-bow lakes and other backwaters of the Cinca, a tributary of the River Ebro. The lure that he swears by, in the muddy river waters, is a wobbling spoon, in conjunction with a flexible spoon of the shad type, which combines the attracting effect of the vibrations of the plastic fish with the silver flashes from the wobbling spoon.

MICHEL NEUVILLE: THE "IRISHMAN" FROM FRANCE

His first trip to Ireland was a revelation for Michel Neuville. He found a country where the people still know how to give the warmest of welcomes to a visiting foreigner, a country of water, heathland, and rocks that are bathed in a fabulous light.

In love with pike fishing, and enraptured by this legendary country, he decided to set up a fishing camp on the banks of the River Erne, in County Cavan, a water preserved in its wild state, and renowned for its very large fish. He considers the best technique to be a deadbait, on a floating mount of the JPK type (a French brand). In this way, the fish lure, weighted higher up the line, but slightly raised off the bottom, does not escape the attention of the predator! It should be pointed out that live bait fishing is banned throughout the Irish Republic.

BERNARD THOMPSON: ALASKA

Bernard Thompson stands out as a veteran in the land of the "last frontier". He is a specialist on salmon, who has fished all the rivers of this state — the largest in the United States. During the closed season for salmon, he has found one of the other riches of the ancestral lands of the

Inuit, the pike, which he fishes for mainly in the winter, beneath the ice. According to him, the best technique is to dangle a metal fish between two waters. This is a practice as old as the hills, one that is marvelously effective when applied to the listless behavior of the fish when the waters are icy.

ALAIN TREMBLAY

On the banks of the Saint Lawrence River, the famous Tremblay family has acquired a legendary reputation for supplying the best fishing and hunting guides in Quebec Province to the various concessionary stores along the river. Alain Tremblay is no exception. He is the owner of the *Le Martin Pêcheur* (Kingfisher) store, and he specializes in fishing for the local pike-perch — the yellow walleye — and the pike, which he tracks down in the most secret backwaters. As a specialist in the use of surface lures, he tracks the pike throughout the summer using an imitation frog — of natural size — fitted with a small battery-operated device that emits croaking noises when animated. His secret is very short recoveries and the fishing of specific stations (usually the most congested), actually those that nobody exploits!

Fishing techniques

The lures now available are so many, and so varied, and capable of fishing all depths, that the technique is one of the most varied and specialized.

CASTING, USING LURES

The range of lures now on sale is so great that this technique can be used to handle all situations, and to fish all levels in the water, from the surface down to great depth. It is, moreover, an active, itinerant practice by which many fishing stations can be tried in record time.

Revolving or wobbling spoons, flexible lures, swimming-fish lures, and other poppers for casting are the basic lures for the pike angler.

Swimming-fish lures

Depending on their density and the angle of the flap, some float and others sink. Within these two categories, there are models that descend more or less rapidly and deeply. Lures of the Rapala type, which are suitable for all waters, are especially effective for surface fishing among weed beds and carpets of water lilies, throughout the summer. The choice will then be for floating lures that sink with a wriggling action when pulled through the vegetation. Where their use is permitted, a swimming-fish lure is a deadly bait for trolling. Irish anglers use it for preference in the large Irish lakes.

Surface lures

Surface lures have been used for decades in North America for all summer fishing for predatory fish. They have recently turned up in Europe, where it has

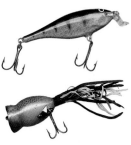

The pike is especially predatory very early in the morning. Swimming-fish lures are very good for catching it.

been realized that the bizarre features of this varied and colorful category are not only of interest for the largemouth bass, but also may attract the attention of a pike lurking in the vegetation along the banks, and arouse its aggressiveness. One of the best known is the spinner fish, originally used for bass fishing, which has proved to be highly effective when fishing for pike. Large poppers for casting, imitation mice and frogs, also have their uses in the dog days, when the pike hunts at the surface for amphibians and other prey crossing the water. Floating swimming-fish lures of the type of crank baits, stick baits, and jerk baits, are also very effective, and easily worked amid the water plants. The chief interest of lures of this type is that they can be used to fish inaccessible places — a corridor of clear water between the lily beds, or the reed stems — where other standard techniques, such as the spoon, are inoperative. They have to be worked in a particular way: once they have reached their destination, they should be left immobile for a few seconds, before being recovered in a series of jerky stops and starts.

It is, in fact, quite like fishing for largemouth bass with a popper. The attack is often highly spectacular at the surface, with the fish leaping out of the water with a splash to seize the lure. Striking too early is a mistake to be avoided — wait a fraction of a second before raising the tip of the rod in a sweeping, heavy movement.

The spinner-fish, originally intended for sea-bass fishing, may sometimes tempt a pike.

Metallic lures

These lures are routinely used in Europe, but less so in North America, where the preference is for flexi-

The pike will readily attack a surface lure throughout the summer.

Fishing techniques

ble lures, swimming-fish, and surface lures.

Lures with a revolving blade are among the basic equipment of spinners. They are not only easy to use, but also versatile, being of two kinds. There are large revolving spoons that rotate with a slow fluttering action at a distance from the axis, which are for shallow water, and which begin to revolve on the slightest prompting – sometimes purely on account of the pressure of the water and the rate of immersion. The other kind are spoons with large, straight blades, which rotate close to the axis, and are better for fishing deep water or where the current is lively. Spoons intended for pike, which end in a triple hook, often have a special device meant to attract the predator and focus its attack. This device may be no more than a tuft of red wool placed round the hook, a soft

plastic tongue, or a tuft of colored hackles.

All revolving spoons are usually meant to be worked alone, but each model has its own optimum rate of recovery at a given depth. The fishing action involves casting close to places where the fish may be assumed to be lying (the edges of reed beds, near an obstacle such as a fallen tree, the line of the bank, or where a branch dips into the water), and then to wind it in slowly, level with the bottom, at the minimum speed at which the blade will rotate.

Animation of the lure involves successive pulling, relaxing, and sideways movements aimed at varying the rate of recovery.

Superb pike, caught by spinning in a pond in the Sologne, in France.

Wobbling spoons

Long regarded as a last resort, and difficult to handle, wobbling spoons are not credited with the success that they deserve. They are excellent lures that wonderfully mimic the clumsy movements of a wounded or sick fish, and glide perfectly when the line is slackened, giving off very attractive reflections. The Irish, in particular, are not in any doubt, and spoons almost of shoehorn size are used to troll the vast loughs of the Emerald Isle, this being thought the best way to catch one of the legendary mammoth pike said to lurk at the bottom.

Various revolving spoons for pike.

There are very large-bladed spoons that dive rapidly, and may be used to fish the deepest and most inaccessible holes. However, there are also very light blades, the merit of which is that they have a far more gliding and unpredictable swimming movement. When weighted in front, they may also be used at great depth. The only constraint on the use of this type of lure, which is not self-operating, is that it must be animated in a particular way, by abrupt pulling and relaxing of the line, and by lateral sweeping of the top of the rod, to simulate the movements of a potential prey in the water.

Flexible lures

When it comes to flexible lures, our American colleagues, the inventors of soft plastic imitations of small water creatures that delude the fish, enchant us with their ingenuity and limitless imagination. The first flexible lures to reach Europe were twists and commas, which were

The wobbling spoon is an excellent lure for trolling for pike.

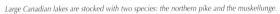

Large Canadian lakes are stocked with two species: the northern pike and the muskellunge.

Fishing techniques

immediately taken up with enthusiasm by pike-perch fishermen.

We should not forget, however, that the Americans originally created these lures for use when fishing for the largemouth bass, which remain the fish of their dreams.

Given that the pike readily behaves in the same way as the largemouth bass, it is clear that such lures will also be able to seduce our pike.

Although the first flexible lures, the well-known commas, were quite unlike anything living in water, there are now many quite realistic imitations of crayfish, and of other small, squid-like creatures with wavy tentacles. Flexible lures have several things to recommend them: they are easy to use, relatively cheap, come in a vast range for use in all situations, and, above all, may be used to fish the most overgrown places. The tip of the hook is either turned upward, or buried in the body of the lure, which significantly reduces the risks of hooking. Flexible lures may be used on the surface (the Slug is an example), or mounted on one of the many variants of a leaded head of Jig type.

Fishing with a manipulated dead fish

Apart from the size of the chosen fish, which is usually larger, the technique is similar to that recommended for the pike-perch, except that all water levels should be fished, and not just the deep water and the bottom layer.

Live bait fishing

Although banned in some countries, including Ireland, this technique is undoubtedly the surest way of catching very large pike. It is – in every sense of the word – a deadly practice, in place of which the technique using a dead fish, known as "sitting dead", may sometimes be tolerated.

Apart from the need to know where the fish are stationed, all that is required is the ability to put together ingenious mounts that will, one day or another, seduce the pike of our dreams!

The live bait has been swallowed deeply.

Pike caught on live bait, with a floating line and a sail float, or insert driver.

Fishing techniques

FLY-FISHING

Fly-fishing for predators in general, and for pike in particular, is a fairly recent introduction, but one that is quite the vogue today. For more than a decade, dedicated fly-fishermen have realized that salmonids are not, by a long way, the only potential victims for this royal technique.

Once again, the Americans initiated the practice of fly-casting for other worthy adversaries — tarpon, bonefish, largemouth bass, peacock bass, and, of course, such predators as the pike, but also the muskellunge, another legendary North American fish. There is, admittedly, a reason for this growing interest in the technique. Firstly, there is the opportunity to continue with a favorite sport during the closed season for salmonids. Above all, the special make-up of streamers for pike, incorporating an anti-weed device, makes it possible to fish the most inaccessible places, and to make a lure move comfortably through the most tangled weed beds.

Flies

True pike flies are usually tied using large feathers mounted on materials of low absorbency, so as to offer the least resistance to the air when damp. In enclosed water and for surface fishing, exact imitations of, for example, mice and small frogs may be used. All streamers for use with greased line or at depth should include synthetic fibers incorporating either tinsel or crystal flash, or alternatively some other modern material.

Fishing action

Fishing is "by sight", at specific lies, or better, when the opportunity exists, in surface pursuits. The selected model is then propelled toward the activity that has been spotted, and worked at various depths, generally near the surface, because the technique is most effective in fairly shallow water. For it to be attractive, the

Streamers for pike are often highly colored.

streamer must also be brought back in an uneven series of movements. The streamer is often attacked more delicately than a surface lure. The hand should hesitate for a moment before striking, after the fisherman has felt the slightest hint of a bite, or felt the merest halt through the butt of the rod.

Spectacular strike on a pike taking a surface fly.

Pike caught on a colored streamer.

Fishing techniques

FISHERIES

MAJOR DESTINATIONS

There are still a few countries that are true paradise for the pike fishing enthusiast. Some of them are far away and costly, while others are far more accessible, both financially, and in terms of distance. Europe itself offers excellent possibilities of a change of environment and guaranteed record catches!

IRELAND

This country has captivated many European anglers during recent decades. It should be said that many travel agencies offer very reasonable, all-inclusive package tours, that good-

sized fish abound, that fish more than 3 feet long are frequently caught, and that, additionally, the change of environment is guaranteed, because of the beauty of the scenery and the warmth of the Irish, who always greet anglers on tour with that special open-hearted welcome that is a feature of their race. Apart from 14,000 well-stocked lakes, including the famous Lough Mask, there are two rivers that should be given priority attention: the Shannon, Ireland's longest river which rises in County Sligo, and the Erne, in County Cavan. It should be remembered that livebait fishing is prohibited in the

Irish Republic. The best techniques are use of a dead fish, inert or manipulated, casting lures, and trolling large wobblers.

NETHERLANDS

Thanks to an impeccable stocking policy, the Dutch canals are very well stocked with pike of all sizes. The country is, therefore, a preferred destination, especially valued by fly-fishermen, who normally use a large streamer, but also a loffer at the surface.

SPAIN

Spanish reservoir lakes, especially in the province of Aragon, have become a

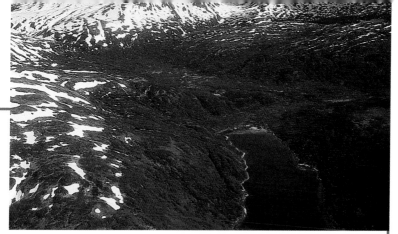

The superb scenery of Alaska, whose many lakes are often stocked with fine northern pike.

destination not to be missed by all who have a passion for predators; they offer record catches of catfish, but also have many largemouth bass, pike-perch, and other fish, including pike! At relatively little cost, just the other side of the Pyrenees, there lies a dream holiday, trying one's skill against trophy fish, but also, by way of a change, trying to add to one's record all the species to be found in this beautiful country.

CANADA

Canada is undoubtedly the best current destination for pike, especially if you have the luck to go to the Great Slave Lake, where record catches are recorded every year, and where the abundance of fish is, quite literally, breath-taking.

Those who speak French should not fail to visit Quebec, where fishing is by permit from the concessionaires. The basin of the Saint Lawrence affords good possibilities for pike, muskellunge and pike-perch.

UNITED STATES

The pike abounds in American waters, especially in the region of the Great Lakes. Those who go to Alaska after salmon may vary their pleasure by pike fishing, mainly in the lakes and rivers (Kobuk, for example, and Noatak) around the Arctic Circle.

A fine catch in a backwater of the Rio Cinco, in Spain.

Biology

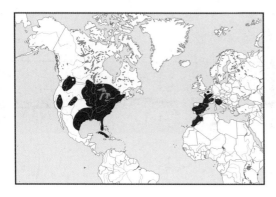

FOREIGN NAMES

French: black-bass à
grande bouche.
German: Forellen-
barsch.
Italian: percisco trota.

This fantastic sport fish, the acrobat of our predators, which responds to being hooked by putting up a formidable display, is exciting, fascinating, spell-binding, and also sometimes discouraging, because it is so temperamental, but never, at all events, to be ignored. And when it makes its bow in a burst of iridescent droplets, the angler is plunged into despair, although it may have satisfied his wildest hopes by deigning to bite firmly on the lure.

For, at the very last moment, it remains in control, and goes through its entire repertoire. Dragonfly or butterfly? Popper, slider, jerk bait, spinner bait? The question is phrased in terms that are flavorsome, exotic, and even mysterious, the alchemy in the book of spells of bass men, which holds the carefully guarded secrets of a brotherhood in quest of its Holy Grail. The task is to deceive the most lunatic, the most unpredictable of our adversaries: this wizard with fins and scales called the largemouth bass.

The English name largemouth comes from the formidable jaws.

LARGEMOUTH BASS *(Micropterus salmoides)*

The largemouth bass, a gregarious fish, congregates where it can easily hide.

DESCRIPTION

The immediate impression on first seeing a largemouth bass is one of the sheer brute force of the fish.

The body is attractively stocky, massive, and covered in ridged scales that appear to form a carapace. Undoubtedly the most impressive feature is the head, which has so deep a mouth slit that it is called the largemouth bass. The disturbing aspect of the fish is reinforced by the overdeveloped lower jaw, which largely overlaps the upper jaw, and is an indication of the basically opportunistic feeding behavior of the species, which will feed on flies, as well as being a predator at great depth.

The other attributes that make it a redoubtable predator are the numerous teeth on the arches of the jaws, and on the tongue, a thick caudal peduncle (the root of the tail), which gives it terrific acceleration, the most perfect balance in the water being assured by a single paired dorsal fin, made up of two connected parts.

The latter detail serves to differentiate the perch from the largemouth bass, which is a member of the family Centrarchidae, the sunfishes, among which are many great sports fish.

A predator to the tips of its fins, the largemouth bass display true coquetry.

GEOGRAPHIC DISTRIBUTION

This fish is a native of the southeastern United States. It occurs naturally in the southern part of the large lakes, and the convex system of waterways in southern Ontario, and Quebec. In the United States, its origins are in the south of the Mississippi, but thanks to large-scale cultivation programs there is now at least one isolated largemouth bass population in almost every American state. In Canada, apart from Ontario

Biology

Perch and largemouth bass hidden beneath a rock, awaiting prey.

peratures between 32 and 86 °F (0–30 °C). Thus, in the northern United States, it is not adversely affected by cold spells lasting for several weeks, while in Florida, the Florida strain flourishes in waters at 86 °F (30 °C). The mean temperature, preferably staying in the range 59–68 °F (15–20 °C), does not slow the development of the fish. The largemouth bass is highly opportunistic in its choice of habitat, and is to be found in many biotopes. In Spain and Morocco, for example, but also in many other countries, it finds its best development conditions in man-made reservoirs, in which it develops among immersed obstacles such as sunken trees,

and part of Quebec, isolated strains are found in British Columbia, Alberta, Saskatchewan, and Manitoba. In France, it is said to have been first introduced in 1882. It has also been successfully introduced into Poland, Switzerland, Italy, Denmark, and Germany. In the reservoir lakes of Spain and Morocco, there is now a veritable explosion of bass, and these two countries have become favored destinations for largemouth bass fishing. It may also be seen in other latitudes, in South Africa, for example, Kenya, and Zimbabwe, and also in Mexico, Honduras, Colombia, Cuba, and the Dominican Republic, Japan, Thailand, and Vietnam. On Madagascar, it literally teems in some waters, such as Lake Aloatra, an

immense swamp covering some 494,000 acres (200,000 hectares).

BEHAVIOR

The extraordinary adaptability of the largemouth bass is explained by the fact that it is a eurythermal fish, able to tolerate a wide range of tem-

An active predator, this largemouth bass ascends on its prey from its hiding place in the reed bed.

A TEMPERAMENTAL AND UNPREDICTABLE FISH

The temperamental nature of the largemouth bass — periods of frenzied feeding alternate with long periods of apathy — is partly explained by its continuous search for a comfortable temperature, not only water temperature, but also the amount of sunlight, which directly affects its feeding patterns and the water levels occupied. In a reservoir lake, in particular, and in the transitional seasons (in Spain, for example), during spring (March) and autumn (October–November), it may hunt to great depths, as deep as 65 feet (20 m)! In the dog-days, on the other hand, it rises close to the surface, although it shuns the sun, hiding in the shade of foliage or water lilies. Still in Spain, echo-sounding has been used to pinpoint the depth at which the fish patrol, as an aid to strategy. A further point is that the largemouth bass will often target a specific prey, which may be dragonflies, crayfish, fish, or something else. If it is only after dragonflies, there is no point in trying worm, for example.

Furthermore, when it is patrolling at depth, looking for small fish, only a swimming-fish lure, or a flexible lure, will make the difference.

The size of lure is also of some importance. On occasion, only the smallest shad will attract its attention (when it is chasing schools of alevins, for example). In other circumstances, large bass will snap up giant American worms, eight inches (20 cm) long. It is up to the angler to be sufficiently observant to achieve success.

Biology

remains of dwellings, or landslide debris. It is a typical inhabitant of calm water at moderate temperatures. In rivers, it systematically occupies inlets, backwaters, and oxbows. It also likes canals, natural lakes, and ponds, provided that there is adequate bank vegetation and floating vegetation, to provide a natural screen for ambushing its prey.

Diet

The wealth of lures created by the Americans for largemouth bass fishing testifies to its great eclecticism concerning food; it feeds on the bottom, between waters, and at the surface on all available prey in its ecosystem. Researchers have noted that fish account for less than 50 percent of its consumption. This bass is primarily a fish-eater early in spring, and again in autumn, when it takes advantage of the thousands of alevins in the water plants along the banks. It is also a deadly hunter of catfish, and is undoubtedly the only predatory fish to eat them. It mainly attacks clusters of alevins, which dart around, mouths wide open, in the middle of the swarm. In summer, when lying in ambush under the weed beds and water lilies, it feeds a lot at the surface, taking any prey — dragonflies hovering at water level, but also water snakes, frogs, newts, small rodents, and even young birds. American catalogs of flies and lures even include imitation terrapins, which is quite logical, as is shown by the following observation. Terrapins were hatching on a sand bank at the edge of the water in a pond in the Bourbonnais. Shortly after, when they sought refuge in the pond, they were marked down by a large bass, which joyfully set about them, while their shells were still soft. Lastly, we should not forget the crayfish, a favorite prey of the bass, and all kinds of worms. Returning to water snakes, large flexible lures with a wobbling tail are a better imitation of the smooth progress of a water snake than of the crawling of a worm. Similarly, the surface lure known as a stick bait, has an undulating swimming motion highly reminiscent of a small grass snake crossing a pond.

The alevins feed mainly on zooplankton (daphnia, cyclops, etc.) until they reach a length of two inches (5 cm). Starting in the first summer (4 in./10 cm), fish-eating takes over.

Having stunned its prey, the bass settles down to swallow it.

LARGEMOUTH BASS (*Micropterus salmoides*)

Submerged vegetation provides the largemouth bass with fine vantage points.

Reproduction

The largemouth bass reproduces from April to June, when water temperature is from 62 to 70 °F (17–21 °C). As in most members of the family Centrarchidae (and of the Cichlidae, to which the peacock bass belongs), there are complex rituals associated with the reproduction of the largemouth bass. The male has the task of building a large nest, 1–1½ feet (30–50 cm) in diameter. To that end, he excavates a depression in a clean substrate of sand and gravel, possibly including some twigs, close to the banks, at a depth of around 1½–4½ feet (50 cm–1.5 m), but as deep as 6 feet (nearly 2 m) when the slope is steep, as in a reservoir lake. The task is performed by contortions of the body, and with the aid of the powerful caudal fin. When it is finished, the exemplary father sets out in search of mates. It should be pointed out that the nest is usually made close to a visual reference point, usually an obstruction submerged under the water: weed bed, tree stump, stone bedding. Having achieved his end — once a female is circling round the nest — the male begins a complicated display, which may last all day long. This is a subtle courtship which entices the chosen one to lay her eggs, roughly 2,300 per pound of body weight (5,000 per kg),

Biology

with an average diameter of ½ in./.5 mm, with a sticky coat that adheres perfectly to the substrate, thus preventing the eggs from dispersing outside the protection of the nest depression. Not only are the eggs laid in batches and immediately fertilized by the male, but in many instances, they come from several spawning females, captivated by the graceful dance of the father fish, who is unusually anxious to ensure the continuation of the species.

A single nest may contain more than 20,000 eggs, which is equivalent on average to the total output of four spawning females.

Another striking aspect of the behavior of this exemplary father is that he keeps a careful watch over "his" eggs, oxygenating them by slow movements of the fins. This procedure also has the aim of preventing the deposition of sediment that might asphyxiate the eggs. He also vigorously ejects any intruder, such as perch or catfish, always looking for pickings.

Unfortunately, such brave charges against any intruder often have a fatal outcome, as when a large pike, arriving in the vicinity of a "nursery", is quick to take advantage of an easy prey, which literally hurls itself, without any forethought, straight into its mouth. Incubation takes an average of 72 hours when water temperature is in the range of 64 to 68 °F

Two separated dorsal fins identify the largemouth bass as a centrarchid.

(18–20 °C). Resorption of the yolk sac takes about 10 days, throughout which time, and for the next two weeks or more, the alevins remain in their comfortable nest, watched over by their father, who will subsequently abandon them.

Thereafter the alevins leave the nest and patrol in swarms along the banks. They are often to be seen clustering in the shade of foliage at river level, where they are a chosen prey for small predators, such as the kingfisher. They then disperse early in the autumn, and form small groups.

Largemouth bass caught with lures.

Fishing techniques

The most capricious of our aquatic adversaries may be caught by spinning and by fly-casting. The lures used are among the most whimsical.

Casting tackle that includes a revolving-spool reel is what bass men like.

SPINNING

Although largemouth bass purists are exclusively fly-fishermen, it has to be admitted that spinning seems, in general, to be a better means of catching this temperamental and opportunistic fish; that is because of the large range of lures currently available, including metallic lures, flexible lures, swimming-fish lures, and poppers to suit all situations and fish at all depths, as required by the season and the behavior of the fish.

Equipment

A baitcasting rod, as recommended by many American and Spanish specialists, who characteristically operate from special bass boats, is the real rod for large-mouth bass fishing. Such rods, usually short, are often in one piece. The butt is shaped for better grip, and usually has a revolving spool reel. A light casting rod, 8–9 feet (2.5–2.7 m) long, with a lure weight of 1–3 ounces/10–30 g, and tip action, may also be used. A good .24-mm diameter line (breaking strength 10–12 lb) is the minimum needed,

The bass boat is fast and specially equipped for bass fishing.

especially when fishing in an overgrown place.

Lures

Flexible lures

The flexible lures that have triumphed in Europe and that have captivated all anglers fishing for predators, were designed in the United States specifically

A fine largemouth bass caught with a flexible lure.

for the largemouth bass. The main point of these lures is their great versatility. Depending on the way in which they are mounted, they can be used at the surface, among the most tangled weed beds, and at depth, when mounted on a weighted head (Jig mounting), a Texan, or a Carolina mount.

Some lures are astonishingly realistic and faithfully copy the swimming or the silhouette of a usual prey of the largemouth bass. Others are more fanciful, but no less effective in some circumstances, because the ability of a flexible lure to attract goes far beyond mere physical resemblance.

It is above all the movement and the mobility of these lures, which have a body, tail, claws, or feet that quiver at the slightest prompting, that attracts the attention of the predator and incite it to attack. Color and smell may also be of importance. Many specialists soak their lures in a solution of an attractant with the aroma of fresh fish or crayfish.

Worms

These lures, which are still called worms, are an essential for fishing in deep water in a reservoir lake. Depending on the design, the worm wriggles to a greater or lesser degree, and the vibrations emitted differ. Most have a comma-shaped tail that wriggles when pulled. Texan or Carolina mounts should be used for deep fishing. The Texan has a sinker directly abutting the hook, while the Carolina has the sinker that comes to a halt at the swivel, to which the free leader, about 8 inches (20 cm) long, is attached. This type of mount is good for use when fishing stony bottoms, when the fish are active, because the lure glides when the line is

LARGEMOUTH BASS *(Micropterus salmoides)*

Slugs are deadly flexible lures for largemouth bass.

slackened, and undulates gently towards the bottom. The tip of the hook (size 2–4) incorporated in the worm is submerged in the mass of the plastic, which greatly reduces the risk of unhooking, but necessitates a sharp, strong strike.

The slug, a type of worm lure, is used for fishing at the surface. It looks like a little lamprey slithering at the surface, and comes into its own during the summer.

Twists and commas

Twists and commas, by far the most universal lures, and the first to come on the market, are very effective on a Jig mounting when the fish are relatively inactive or concentrating on alevins. The indispensable shads, duds, and sandros are included in this category.

Crayfish

The crayfish is a part of the staple diet of the largemouth bass. The many models commercially available have claws and pincers that move very attractively at the slightest impulse. The crayfish combines the undulating movements of a twist with a most captivating silhouette. The lure is usually soaked in an attractant solution naturally smelling of crayfish! Such treatment has the special value of reducing failed strikes, because the fish holds the plastic creature with an appetizing smell longer in its mouth.

Salamander

This is a lure much favored by Spanish anglers in reservoir lakes. The highly realistic silhouette looks just like a salamander, or a newt, prey greatly liked by the bass. The salamander

A crayfish lure soaked in a shellfish attractant is good for bass fishing.

A proud fisherman with his catch, on the Ebro, in Spain.

Fishing techniques

The salamander is another good lure.

may be used at the surface, with an ordinary hook with the point buried in the plastic, or when fishing at depth, attached to a Texan or Carolina mount.

FISHING WITH METALLIC LURES
Lures
Spoons
These are combination lures, in which one or more rotating or wobbling spoons are associated with flexible lures of the comma type, or with kinds of small, many-tentacled squid-like lures. The best-known model is the spinner bait. It is also standard practice to use a 2–4 inch (5–10 cm) wobbler which weighs ⅛th –⅝th oz (5–20 g).
Preference should be given to heavy, colored models at the start of the season (red, yellow fluo, etc.), dressing the hook with hackles or thin plastic strips. Rotating spoons, better adapted to

summer fishing, may also be colored and fanciful; select from the range in sizes 2 and 3. Having regard to the strength of the jaws of the large-mouth bass, strong iron hooks should always be used.

Swimming fish
There are several score of models, floating or diving, and all gaudy. They can be used for fishing at the surface, among weed beds, and at depth.
From among the typically American models, we may mention the stick bait, which has no flap. This simple balsa stick glides silently over the surface, imitating a reptile or even an amphibian moving unobtrusively among the water lilies. The Jerk bait is one of the most effective lures when largemouth bass — pike or muskellunge — are hunting at the surface. Its sinuous, erratic, and unpredictable swimming movements are very like those of a water snake, because the

front end of the lure is shaped to make it move to left and right when pulled. It is used mainly in the weed beds of ponds, or under overhanging branches on the edge of a reservoir lake.
The popper with flap, or crawler, has a flap curiously mounted at the front of the lure, which is boisterous and makes a lot of splashing. The popper for spinning was designed for the largemouth bass. Depending on the angle at which the lure is set (concave, or with the front face beveled), it pops, or makes great splashes, when

A bass taken with a Rapala among reed beds.

LARGEMOUTH BASS *(Micropterus salmoides)*

FISHING AT THE SURFACE: THE STOP AND GO TECHNIQUE

When there is considerable activity by bass at the surface, Americans swear by the "stop and go" technique. The largemouth bass is known to be curious, and at times temperamental, and so on, but it often knows how to be extremely wary. This simple technique will sometimes catch it off guard. As soon as the floating lure reaches its destination, whether it be a swimming fish, a popper, a stick bait, or a lure bait, it should be left immobile for some little time, before dragging it for, say, 18 inches (45 cm), followed by a pause. What should then be done is to make it tremble slightly *in situ*. The largemouth bass, alerted by the fall of the lure, will be circumspect. Then the object is animated, and twirls at the surface, before stopping again, and becoming inert. Sometimes it seems to be writhing in the last throes.

To sum up, the predator comes to regard it as a prey in difficulty that it is, at last, going to swallow!

---

pulled. Nor, or course, should we forget swimming-fish lures of the Rapala type, or revolving fish.

A deep-diving swimming-fish lure.

FLY-FISHING

The largemouth bass, which hunts at the surface throughout the summer months, attacking dragonflies and other land insects, may be caught by fly-fishing, provided that what we mean by fly is an unlikely collection imitating almost all the usual prey of the bass. These are often wonders of ingenuity, which is a part of the pleasure of this kind of fishing, in which the most whimsical models are found alongside aston-

ishingly realistic imitations. This is a further proof of the temperamental nature of this fish, which is often inclined to seize lures that to all intents and purposes would appear to have come straight out of the wildest imagination of a writer of science fiction!

Equipment

This should be robust, for a number of reasons. Firstly, the adversary is combative and nervous, makes splashes at the surface in its

desperate rushes, and dives powerfully, often right in the middle of obstacles such as water lilies, submerged trees, and other aquatic vegetation, which it must be forced to leave. The size and density of the lures is another reason why it is necessary to have sturdy and reliable equipment.

A good compromise is a 9-foot reservoir or light salmon rod, possibly with a butt grip, adapted to take a no. 7 or no. 8 self-floating line. Special attention must

Fishing techniques

This bass did not resist the attraction of a well-presented popper.

the largemouth bass, it is worthwhile having a wide range of more or less realistic models of the usual prey of the fish, including gaudy creations, such as the popper, and very unobtrusive models, such as a dragonfly, or a large sedge.

Poppers
Give the Devil his due! Although the ancestor of largemouth bass lures is sometimes disappointing, it may make the difference. The balsa wood lure has several profiles: a front face beveled toward the point (it ricochets on the water), or toward the rear (it plunges

be paid to the leader, which should be very short for a streamer, no more than 8–10 feet (2.5–3 m). On the other hand, when dealing with very choosy fish, using dry fly or a small popper, a longer tapering leader will be found to be more sophisticated. The following is an established formula, which works very well: 15 in. (20 cm) of .4 mm, 15 in. (40 cm) of .35 mm, 14 in. (35 cm) of .30 mm, 12 in. (30 cm) of .26 mm, and 24 in (70 cm) of .24–.22 mm diameter line.

Flies, streamers, and poppers
Flies
Taking ito account the highly diversified diet of

Fishing with a float-tube under overhanging branches on the bank.

gently), or a concave front face, in which case the popper gives off a cloud of bubbles when it is pulled. The popper may be made of goat hair. Its silhouette will invariably be vaguely suggestive of a frog with protruding eyes, or a large insect.

The ability of the lure to attract is increased by the addition of small mobile feet, which tremble when animated, and a "tail" of feathers, which undulate at the surface of the water.

The most whimsical colors are used, depending on the imagination of each individual. One important

The popper has been delicately positioned on a water lily leaf, before being animated.

detail: in over-fished waters, wherever the bass has learned to mistrust a gaudy lure, the size of lure should be reduced.

All retailers stock wonderful series of minute poppers that vaguely imitate a beetle or a small frog, etc., which also deceive fine reservoir trout.

Flies used at the surface

Let us pass from the gaudy popper to the small object made from feathers or hair that is placed discretely on the water, and then glides silently, like a slider. Bombers, muddler min-

Fishing techniques

nows, sedges, bumble bees, all of which are usually made of rooster hackles or goat hair, are very suitable for largemouth bass fishing, when the fish are mainly taking insects, or have learned to treat the popper with caution. The "box of tricks" certainly ought to include an imitation dragonfly, and especially the blue or red damsel fly (from the *Agrion* species).

Other surface imitation lures
The mouse, which works in rather the same way as the popper, although it is far less boisterous, merely gliding on the water without any splashing, is very successful for catching because small aquatic rodents are a part of the daily diet of the largemouth bass. Other suggestions could include a realistic imitation of a frog, and even a terrapin.

Streamers
The largemouth bass has got itself quite a reputation for hunting at the surface in the summer. Nevertheless, it is very likely to patrol at depth during the dog days, depending on the circumstances (luminosity, water and air temperature, time of day), which is its custom when climatic conditions are extreme (frost or great heat).

Prowess is not always a matter of years, as is shown by this superb largemouth bass caught by a young angler.

LARGEMOUTH BASS *(Micropterus salmoides)*

SMALLMOUTH BASS *(MICROPTERUS DOLOMIEU)*

The smallmouth bass, like the largemouth, is recognized by all sports anglers for its fighting spirit. When hooked, it puts on a really spectacular acrobatic performance, sometimes leaping out of the water like a dolphin, hitting out with its tail to rid itself of the lure that holds it prisoner. Although the American record, established in Dale Hollow Lake (Kentucky) is 11 pounds 15 ounces (5.42 kg), the average weight is one to two pounds (500g–1 kg). Initially, the smallmouth bass was found only in eastern North America. Today, it is encountered in most American States, in Nova Scotia, New Brunswick, Manitoba, British Columbia, and Saskatchewan. The

indigenous populations in southern Ontario and Quebec have spread to Timmins, in Ontario, and Hull, in Quebec. In Europe, it had been introduced into France, on the Belgian frontier, but the populations seem nearly extinct. Given the smaller size of its jaws, the smallmouth bass has to make do with small prey: insects, crayfish, amphibians, and alevins, apparently with a preference for crustaceans. Unlike the largemouth bass, it prefers rivers with lively, oxygenated currents, and a pebble bed, or lakes with clear water and much landslide debris. The same tackle as has been recommended for trout may be used in fly-fishing or spinning for it.

Other bass species
There are some other less well-known species in American waters. The redeye bass, *Micropterus coosae*; the spotted bass, *Micropterus punctulatus,* in the basin of the Mississippi and the Ohio, which has two subspecies, *Micropterus punctulatus kenskalli* and *Micropterus punctulatus wichitae*; the Guadelupe bass, *Micropterus treculi,* found only in Texas, and the Suwannee bass, *Micropterus notius,* which lives in Florida and Georgia.

Moreover, depending on its mood, it sometimes abandons the search for its usual prey (frogs, insects), to go after alevins on the bottom, or among the aquatic vegetation along the banks. Streamers are then indis-

pensable, in the awareness that exact copies of small fish do not necessarily make the difference, as the most temperamental of our predatory coarse fish do not hesitate, under certain circumstances, to bite at multi-

colored plumes quite unlike the silhouette of any water creature.

Fishing techniques

Sometimes, the largest bass will take only minute poppers.

Fishing action

The most diverting approach is fishing by sight. The fish may be located during the summer by their dark silhouettes just below the surface. They appear to be drowsy, seemingly detached from the mysteries of aquatic life, the busy life being lived out near the bottom or in mid water. The predator bites at a prey on the surface, a dragonfly come to lay its eggs, or a frog unhappily falling from a water lily leaf. The whip cast reaches out toward the stalking predator. The sedge, or the popper, lands delicately, and then the calm surface of the water is disturbed by small concentric ripples. This sends the signals — prey and attack. The popper, or the sedge, is seized in a lightning attack. The angler strikes. There is a flurry of spray, the ebony silhouette of the bass and its bronze flanks finally appear in a pirouette worthy of the finest acrobats.

The fish reveals its identity: a small bundle of muscles, a mouth unfortunately out of proportion, pierced by the hook. In the best instances, the play lasts for some time, but ends in the landing net.

Look at this wonderful adversary, whose only mistake was to let itself be deceived by someone not of its world, someone with the tackle capable of overcoming the wariness of the curious silhouette lying along the bank.

WAYS OF ACTIVATING SURFACE LURES

Walking the dog (zigzagging): the zigzag motion is imparted by short pulls of the end of the rod, in the course of recovering the lure.

Long slide: the lure is recovered by long, slow pulls. The swimming fish glides gently to left and right.

Short jerk: the lure is stationary (obliquely positioned, head out of the water). Give a short, sharp pull. The lure dives, then resurfaces with a wobbling motion.

Stop and go: pausing for a few seconds may prompt the bass to attack. The stop and go technique is one of alternating pulls and rests.

Biology

DESCRIPTION
This percid, originally from central Europe and the East but now found in various parts of North America, is identifiable by its head, which is fine, conical, and extended by a gently convex back, which is not massive, unlike the pike. The broadly slit mouth has needle-sharp teeth of varying

The pike-perch has a preference for great depths and semi-darkness.

PIKE-PERCH *(Stizostedion lucioperca)*

The retina of the pike-perch is perfectly adapted to twilight vision.

sizes, some of which qualify as canines. The generally blue-green eyes show the pike-perch to be a predator that lives in the semi-darkness of great depths, where it retains excellent eyesight thanks to the many rod cells in the retina.

Like all members of its family, it has two separate dorsal fins, the first supported by spiny rays, the second by soft rays. The colors of the pike-perch vary in brightness and continuity with the habitat. There are invariable fine transverse dark stripes on the flanks, not always as distinct as the zebra markings of the perch. The largest fish may reach 30–40 pounds (15 kg) in weight and be more than three feet (1 m) long.

GEOGRAPHIC DISTRIBUTION

The pike-perch occurs widely throughout Europe, with a distribution range extending from the Elbe to the Amsu Dario in Bulgaria. It is also plentiful in large rivers such as the Danube, the Dnieper, and the Don. Since the 1970s, the pike-perch has spread widely in

The pike-perch likes abrupt changes in gradient and rockslides.

southern Europe, and its numbers in many Spanish lakes have risen dramatically. Although present in the British Isles following first introduction around 1910 and several additional introductions, it is not plentiful there.

BEHAVIOR

The eyes of the pike-perch, adapted to poor lighting conditions, indicate that it shuns very strong light. That explains why it goes down deep on sunny days, and hides in the semi-darkness.

In rivers, it differs from all other predatory coarse fish in its liking for zones of currents, where it goes to hunt in the twilight, especially in the summer. It is also to be found below engineering works such as spillways and sluice gates, in the slow eddies formed at the height of every large excavated bank, and wherever the bottom is littered with obstacles.

Biology

When ready to spawn, the pike-perch seeks out zones of water plants.

In reservoir lakes, one of the preferred places for the pike-perch, the fish occupy specific known lies: near submerged trees, rock-slides, buildings submerged by the reservoir, all abrupt changes in gradient, and the platforms preceding the greatest depths, and the cliff line. The pike-perch feeds mainly on such fish as bleak, roach, gudgeon, min-nows, and small chub, etc., with dead prey preponder-ating in its diet. The female reaches sexual maturity at an age of 3–5 years, when it is about 15 inches (40 cm) long, the male at an age of 2–4 years, when it is about 2 inches (5 cm) shorter. The fish seems to be even more demanding than the perch regarding water tempera-ture, which must reach 59 °F (15 °C) before egg-laying is triggered. It also exhibits strict requirements regard-ing choice of spawning ground, which is always on a very clean bottom of sand and fine gravel, or at root level in submerged vegeta-tion. The eggs, about 90,000 per pound of body weight (200,000 per kg) are laid in a kind of rudimen-tary nest prepared by the male, and take 5–7 days to incubate. Throughout that period, the male stands guard, mercilessly chasing schools of small coarse fish before charging.

WALLEYE
(STIZOSTEDION VITREUM VITREUM)

The walleye, one of the most popular predatory coarse fish with American anglers, is very like the European pike-perch, apart from the well-known white spot on the lower lobe of the tail fin, and the undoubtedly brighter color of its tail. Its average size is greater than that of the European pike-perch — the world record stands at 25 pounds (11.3 kg) for a fish caught in Lake Old Hickory, in Tennessee — and it is found widely in the eastern United States, as far as Alabama. In Canada, it is most common in Ontario and Quebec. It may occupy various biotopes, lakes, ponds, rivers, where it feeds on fish, worms, crayfish, and sometimes insects. It spawns in the spring, in relatively shallow water. The walleye is fished by spinning, using lures — revolving spoons and flexible lures — often in conjunction with a bait. Swimming fish of the Rapala type are highly thought of for trolling. Sports anglers generally use a live bait. When it is patrolling relatively shallow water, some specialists even use flies, or streamers, with a sinking line. The most successful artificials are Mickey Finn, Grey Ghost, and Yellow Drak.

Fishing techniques

Albert Drachkovitch is the craftsman of modern pike-perch fishing. His famous invention is invaluable for devotees of the manipulated dead fish technique.

The famous Drachkovitch articulated dead bait flight, with interchangeable weight.

This fish, which fascinates many anglers and is much sought after by gourmets world-wide, has been so often fished for in the past that its wariness has become a byword, so much so that many specialists now assert that, "it doesn't bite any more!" This extreme caution on the part of the pike-perch explains why increasingly sophisticated techniques have now been brought into play to catch it.

FISHING WITH A MANIPULATED DEAD FISH

This technique received its letters patent of nobility in France, to be precise in 1967, thanks to two great specialists — Albert Drachkovitch and Henri Limouzin — who invented the well-known dead bait flight with interchangeable weight and articulated at the head, known as the Drachko flight. It has two size 8–10 triple hooks and a curved needle for insertion into the mouth of the fish, which is already held firmly in position by a strand of brass wire passed round the body behind the head, and wound off in front of the head. This model can be animated in a most effective way and its swimming is perfectly natural. Care must be taken over the

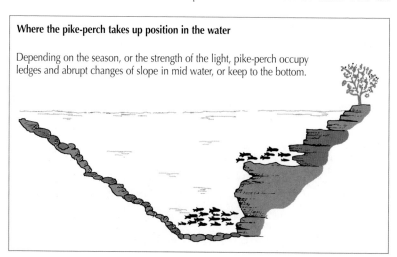

Where the pike-perch takes up position in the water

Depending on the season, or the strength of the light, pike-perch occupy ledges and abrupt changes of slope in mid water, or keep to the bottom.

This magnificent pike-perch was lying under overhanging branches along the bank, in very shallow water.

choice of material, so as to be able to feel the lightest touch at great depth: a stiff rod, 8–9 feet (2.5–2.7 m) long, with marked tip action, which will also transmit the nervousness and the sweep of the movements imparted to the dead fish and ensure effective striking at a distance. Any abnormal pulling or displacement can be seen by the fluo nylon line used. In conjunction with the rod, it is, as a matter of fact, the eyes of the angler.

The fishing action involves maintaining light contact with the nylon line, by placing the index finger lightly on the spool throughout the immersion phase. So doing maintains a slight tension on the line,

A small boat is often needed to track down the pike-perch in its most secret haunts.

Fishing techniques

which is unwound slowly, spiral by spiral.
The slightest halt in the descent, the most infinitesimal lateral displacement of the nylon, may indicate a touch, the signal for an immediate strike! Arrival at the bottom is indicated by a slight loosening of the line. The fish may then be left motionless for a few instants, after which recovery is begun, by sharply raising the tip of the rod, holding the rod high, and proceeding by a series of slight accelerations followed by short pauses. There is no absolute rule about this animation, the point of which is to create the illusion of life. Pulling and relaxing movements are supplemented by lateral shifts of the rod, variations in recovery rate, and dangling movements effected without moving position, directly below the boat.

The reward for what is sometimes several days spent patiently at the water's edge: a large pike-perch taken with a manipulated dead fish.

Fishing techniques

The layout for sliding fishing

The lead shoe stirs up an attractive cloud of sediment. Note that the raised rig prevents snagging on the bottom.

SLIDING FISHING

This new technique is perfectly suited to fishing for pike-perch. What is new about it is the use of highly sensitive rods, the top section of which has a quiver tip. Old-time country fishermen have long practiced this kind of fishing, using the simplest of rigs, a small weight (⅓–½ oz/10–15 g) on a swivel, joined to a trace carrying an ordinary hook (size 2–6). The fishing action involves dragging the bait – a dead fish, or a live fish with shining scales – very slowly and irregularly on the bottom,

Animating a manipulated dead fish at the bottom

pausing from time to time to deceive the pike-perch.

Animating the Drachkovitch manipulated dead fish

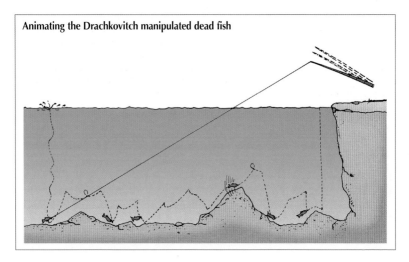

Reservoir lakes are very good places for pike-perch.

FISHING WITH AN INERT DEAD FISH

In the section on the biology of the pike-perch we saw that the predator, having charged into a cloud of alevins, returns later to gather up its catch of dead fish on the bottom. This explains the interest in the present technique, which involves immobilizing a drawn fish on the bottom in the most cluttered spots, by means of a suitable rig; British raised rigs, in which a polystyrene bead is used, are just the thing.

LIVE BAIT FISHING WITH A FLOAT

Many live baits interest the pike-perch: because of its silver scales, which give off multiple reflections, the bleak is an excellent live bait for use in all zones plunged into semi-darkness, and at great depth. It has a heavy oxygen consumption, is difficult to transport, and not able to withstand temperatures above 59 °F (15 °C). Furthermore, it tends to return systematically to the surface, and therefore to become exhausted rapidly. Among the other good live baits, there is the gudgeon, recommended for all fishing with a float, which strives to reach the bottom, unlike

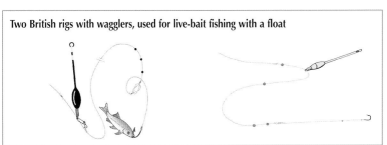

Two British rigs with wagglers, used for live-bait fishing with a float

Fishing techniques

This pike-perch in a reservoir succumbed to the temptation of a well handled Vitala.

the bleak, and the minnow, for use with very thin lines, and the roach, which is restless, resistant, and swims for hours after having been put on the hook.

The goldfish seems an ideal live bait; it is resistant as well as being extremely conspicuous. Because the pike-perch lives at great depths, it must be fished with a floating line, using specific, well-adapted rigs: British rigs with wagglers, or classical float fishing with a sliding float, for fishing the desired depths without too much trouble.

FISHING WITH FLEXIBLE LURES

The flexible lure is highly valued by pike-perch specialists. The range of models on sale is sufficiently wide for all situations, they are easy to use, and not very expensive; these are all arguments in their favor. Twists and commas were the first from the United States to come onto the European market, but there are now many forms, such as shad and sandras which more realistically imitate small fish.

There are two main types of flight for the flexible lure: the weighted head, which the Americans call the Jig, and possibly a mini-Drachko for small fish.

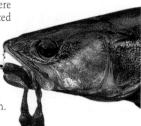

The pike-perch takes flexible lures well if they are made to move lowly.

SAUGER
(STIZOSTEDION CANADENSE)

***Common names in
Quebec:
perche-chien, black
bonhomme, doré
charbonnier.***

Apart from size — the
sauger being smaller than
the walleye — there are
few morphological
characters by which to
distinguish between the
two, which frequently
interbreed. The clear mark
at the end of the lower lobe
of the tail fin in the walleye
is absent from the sauger,
which also has two dorsal
fins typically covered in
black dots, not found in the
walleye. The largest sauger
caught was in North
Dakota, in Lake
Sakakawea. It weighed 8
pounds 2 ounces (4 kg).
Most fish caught weigh
about 2 pounds (1 kg). In
the United States, the
sauger is a typical
inhabitant of large lakes, to
as far as Louisiana, and of
the River Tennessee, in
Alabama. In Canada, its
distribution range is
restricted to southeastern
Quebec, and the southern
half of the prairie
provinces. Strangely, it is
found only in large natural
and man-made waters,
with turbid, deep water. It
spawns in June, and is
mainly a fish-eater.
Lures, especially
conspicuous ones, in
which a live bait is
associated with a revolving
spoon bait with a weighted
head (the Walleye killer of
Mepps, or Eric Dearie), are
the main means of fishing
for the sauger
It may also be
fished in the
standard way
with a flexible
lure baited with
a worm.

The world record for a sauger is held in the United States.

Biology

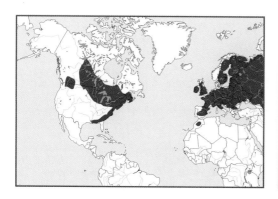

FOREIGN NAMES

*French: perche
commune.*
German: Barsch.
Spanish: perca.

The perch is also known in French as the *perdrix des eaux douces* (freshwater partridge), because of the delicacy of its flesh. The zebra stripes on its flanks have also earned it the nicknames of "the zebra fish" and "the tigress". These

It is called the zebra fish because of the transverse stripes on its flanks.

names are indicative of the interest shown in it by anglers, on several grounds: its abundance, which means regular catches, but also its good appetite, curiosity and aggressiveness. The pleasure of perch fishing is increased by the fact that all sporting techniques, including fly-fishing, may be used.

DESCRIPTION

The perch may be identified by its predominantly greenish flanks with five to seven vertical zebra stripes. The presence of two separate dorsal fins, the first of which is supported by 13–15 spiny rays — capable of inflicting painful wounds — and the second by soft rays, shows it to be a member of the family Percidae. Its stocky, massive body is protected by scales of a special type that feel thick and ridged. These denticulate ctenoid scales are very firmly set, and difficult to remove; special tools are sometimes needed when scaling a fish for cooking. A cheap and highly effective scaler used in the countryside is made by nailing beer-bottle tops with

Its widely open mouth shows it to be a ferocious little predator.

crimped edges onto a plank. The jaws of the perch, set with numerous small teeth, as are the vomer and the palate, leave no doubt about the feeding behavior of the fish: it is exclusively a predator.

The livery differs with the biotope. In running water and in lakes with very clear water, its colors are bright; in particular, the pelvic, pectoral, anal, and caudal fins are a superb bright red. In stagnant water (ponds) it is more darkly colored. The proliferation of perch in a water may lead to dwarfism. Wherever development conditions are favorable and food abundant, the average weight is 7 to 8 ounces (200 g), but some fish may well weigh more than 6½ pounds (3 kg).

GEOGRAPHIC DISTRIBUTION

The perch is common throughout the British Isles and on the European mainland, from Scandinavia to the eastern countries, and in Germany, France, and Spain. It is also plentiful in Morocco. In the United States it is found along the eastern coast, from Maine to northern Florida, and in Alabama. Its distribution range also extends far to the west, well beyond the Appalachians. In Canada, it is found widely in New Brunswick, Nova Scotia, Quebec (where it is called the *perchaude*), Ontario, Manitoba, Saskatchewan, and Alberta. The perch populations in British Columbia are much smaller.

BEHAVIOR

Although the perch is generally common in natural lakes and man-made reservoirs, it also colonizes most other aquatic biotopes — large, medium, and small rivers and streams, where it always turns up, and even high-altitude lakes with

Biology

very cold water. Whatever the ecosystem occupied, the fish makes only one demand: that there should be obstacles for its concealment, be they stone blocks, submerged trees, water plants, undercut banks permeated with roots, or engineering works such as the piles of bridges and wooden structures. In reservoir lakes, it develops among any submerged ruins and drowned trees. The nickname "freshwater tigress" given to the perch does not refer merely to the zebra stripes on its flanks, but also to its ferocious appetite. The adult is an opportunistic predator, which also feeds on alevins and various larvae, while juveniles indifferently consume all the small invertebrates of the river, but apparently with a clear preference for mayfly larvae.

When feeding most actively, the perch is exceptionally voracious and continues to kill prey even when replete, not to say bursting! When it hunts in groups, the speed of its reflexes is needed for success in the quest for food, in the face of stiff competition. The largest perch, weighing around 2–6½ pounds (1–3 kg), are solitary predators, and concentrate on catches that are sometimes unexpected, such as chub and roach up to 8 inches (20 cm) long, being used as live bait for pike! The perch is exceptionally prolific. As with

The perch sometimes ventures into the shallows when hunting fry.

This perch, her abdomen distended by eggs, has not lost her appetite.

The perch does not hesitate to venture among scree and other rocky bottoms.

many other fishes, it is water temperature that triggers its reproductive processes. Depending on latitude and height above sea level, the required temperature of around 53–57 °F (12–14 °C) is reached in April, May, or June. The eggs take the curious form of long adhesive tapes deposited on bank vegetation — water plants, submerged branches. Although the eggs are minute (diameter less than ⅒th in./2 mm), they are very numerous; an 8 inch (20 cm) perch may lay 200,000 eggs. This explains why the perch population tends to become excessive, especially in man-made waters. That does not seem to affect the fish, except that there may be indications of dwarfism where population density is very high.

The perch is fundamentally a gregarious fish, whose schooling behavior is to assemble in groups, usually fish of the same size and age. The size of the groups varies with the age of the fish; the younger the fish, the denser the school. Conversely, the largest perch are either solitary, or live in small groups of from two to five. The large perch schools to be seen in alpine lakes form real societies, in which the relations between individuals are governed by very strict rules, with each fish occupying a precise place in the group. In the summer, when there are thousands of alevins patrolling at the surface, the perch form "hunting packs" to pursue their prey, which are encircled and submit, powerless to withstand the murderous onslaughts.

Fishing techniques

The perch is an insatiable predator, interested in anything that shines, moves, or wriggles. The use of lures is, therefore, a most effective way of fishing.

Although the perch does not reach any great size, anglers show a keen interest in it because of the quality of its flesh. Fried perch fillets are a culinary specialty of many countries or regions.

SPINNING

Because the perch is attracted by anything that shines and wriggles, it may be tempted successfully with lures. Flexible lures are used for great depths. The shad or the twist work wonders when mounted on their weighted heads, with a hook with the point turned upward, which reduces the risk of unhooking in cluttered places.

Colors should be changed regularly. For some unexplained reason, the perch attacks only white lures in some waters, and yellow or red lures in others. The flexible lure must be worked for a long time, directly under the rod, at the end of recovery, with a dangling action. This technique will often decide a large perch, which has followed without having decided to attack, to bite. Standard metallic lures are better for fishing rivers and shallow ponds. Small revolving spoons (sizes 0–2), such as the Mepps,

A perch that fell for a flexible lure, the crayfish.

The tin fish, or some other lure for dangling, is one of the best, and the oldest, perch lures.

Tori, and Panther Martin spoons, work miracles. Shining hackles placed on the hook, or a small flexible lure, may make the whole difference.

Perch specialists in North America readily combine a small lure, the reflections of which "beat the retreat", with an earthworm, some distance away.

Light casting equipment, with a lure weight of about ¼–¾ ounces (3–10 g), is perfectly suitable.

DANGLING

These very old techniques, which are often overlooked, are highly effective. Dangling is a technique greatly valued in North America by specialists on fishing through a hole in the ice. The rig usually includes a lure — a revolving spoon — with a split ring connecting

the hook to the blade. The procedure makes unhooking easier. The spoon may be used on its own, or in conjunction with a worm on a short trace. In Europe, especially in France, use is made of the traditional tin fish, an imitation alevin that flashes brightly when worked by the angler.

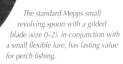

Although the fishing action is simple, in principle it does require some dexterity. The lure is initially allowed to sink to the bottom. A slight loosening of the lines shows that it has reached the bottom. The excess line is then taken in, until the tip of the rod is about 18 inches (50 cm) above the surface. Then the rod is raised by about three feet (80 cm) in the same movement, ending in a strong strike. The lure is then sent down

The standard Mepps small revolving spoon with a gilded blade (size 0–2), in conjunction with a small flexible lure, has lasting value for perch fishing.

A large fish that fell for a whimsical revolving spoon, in conjunction with a tuft of hackles round the triple hook.

again, controlling it so that it glides. An attack is felt as a very clear shock in the butt of the rod, the response to which is to strike immediately. The revolving spoon blade and the live bait or worm may be replaced by the nickel-plated ball used by large-mouth bass specialists on a Texan or Carolina rig.

FLY-FISHING

When using a simple trout rod with a self-floating line, this is a very entertaining procedure for catching large numbers of perch in shallow water. The predominantly blue or orange streamers normally used on long-shank hooks (size 6–8) have golden tinges (tinsel

strands) to simulate the scales of an alevin. The fishing action involves casting the lure to where the fish are assumed to be stationed, and then bringing it back slowly at bottom level, alternately pulling, relaxing, and agitating the stationary lure, to imitate the hesitancy of a small fish in difficulty.

FISHING WITH A FLOATING LINE, USING A MAYFLY LARVA

The larva of a large mayfly (*Ephemera danica* or *vulgata*) is regarded as a treat by the perch. Why then, it may be asked, should one bother with other baits? The answer is quite practical. It is very difficult to collect enough of these small creatures, which are highly

demanding as regards water quality. The larvae generally live in the sand or silt of calm stretches of the river filtering the substrate where they may be collected with a fine-mesh net. Very light rigs are to be recommended when fishing with mayfly larvae: a sensitive, spindle-shaped float, with flexible graduated

Mixed lures, in which a revolving spoon is used in conjunction with marabou fibers or strips of rubber, make good perch lures.

weights. The larva is then baited on a fine iron hook (size 16).

GOOD PERCH STATIONS

The largest perch are to be seen at considerable depth in the river — undercut banks, sheer retaining walls with considerable amounts of riprap, the vicinity of submerged trees, downstream from bridge piles, and any obstacles that split the main current, but also backwaters abounding in vegetation, bights, and calm stretches, and reaches. In ponds, perch readily conceal themselves along the embankment, especially if trees on the bank provide shady areas and submerged roots provide resting places and concealment for ambushing. They also patrol along reed beds, and around landing stages built on piles. In reservoir lakes, the inflow point of a tributary is a favored place, especially in summer, as are the areas around submerged trees, remains of buildings buried by the reservoir waters, scree, and cliffs.

Biology

The wels catfish, originally from central Europe, is now invading the whole of the west and south of the continent. It is now the king of Spanish waters.

The six barbels of the wels catfish are gustatory and chemical receptors.

The wels catfish, one of the greatest challenges for an angler in Europe, is spreading at a rapid rate in southern Europe. It provides a new opportunity for those who love strong sensations and catching trophy fish.

DESCRIPTION

The wels catfish looks rather like American catfish (channel cats), but with some differences, because it belongs to the family Siluridae, rather than to the Ictaluridae.

Unlike the channel cat, it lacks adipose fins, and its large, slightly flattened head has six, rather than eight, barbels: four short ones on the lower jaw, and two large ones on the upper jaw, close to the labial commissure. These two barbels are true chemosensory organs that provide the fish with information on the signals received: including vibrations and chemical olfactory–gustatory (smell and taste) messages. The taste receptors are particularly efficient: they enable the catfish to detect substances dissolved in water with a sensitivity 100,000 times greater than that of our sense of smell.

The highly developed hearing of the wels catfish enables it to receive the most attenuated acoustic information (vibrations, waves, imperceptible pressure variations in the water). The inner ear is highly sophisticated, and the Weberian apparatus, with its fused ossicles, is among the most highly perfected to be seen in fish. This dweller in semi-darkness has many other devices for the detection of a prey or for sensing potential danger.

The lateral line contains many olfactory–gustatory cells (also found elsewhere on the body), and the swim bladder plays a part in the amplification and transmission of acoustic vibrations. It is, therefore, a real living

Biology

In the winter, large numbers of wels catfish tend to congregate in deep holes.

radar, but also a formidable predator, a hunter in darkness, capable of the most terrifying bursts of speed, thanks to its powerful, fan-shaped pectoral fins, rounded caudal fin and, above all, an immense anal fin, supported by more than 90 soft rays and extending along more than half of the lower part of the body. Its body, which is snakelike and protected by a wealth of sticky mucus, also assists it in propulsion.

The head is large, bulky, with a deeply slit mouth and strong grinding jaws, from which few prey escape. The fish has an astonishing propensity for sucking and hanging on. Body color is variable; usually a dark back, contrasting with lighter, marbled flanks. Some albino fish are completely lemon yellow!

In French waters, it is now not uncommon to find wels catfish weighing around 170 pounds (nearly 80 kg). Although these are without any doubt monstrous great fish, they appear tiny by comparison with some giants of around 650 pounds (300 kg) reported caught in central Europe, in the basins of the Dnieper and the Danube.

GEOGRAPHIC DISTRIBUTION

The wels catfish is now well represented in a large part of Europe. Although its expansion into France, Italy, and Spain has been quite recent, it has long been present in other European countries: in Great Britain (introduced at the beginning of the 20th century) and in the Netherlands. A little further east, in Germany, the population is autochthonous (aboriginal). Continuing in the same direction, one comes close to the original cradle of the species in the basins of the Black Sea, the Caspian, and the Aral Sea. Lastly, there are small populations in Scandinavia, especially in some Swedish rivers, but also reaching out into the Baltic Sea.

BEHAVIOR

Given that the wels catfish is found from central Europe to the lakes of Spain, it is obvious that it has astonishing capacity for adaptation to many different biotopes.

Even so, its metabolism, which directly affects its behavior, is temperature-conditioned. The connec-

tion is striking in the catfish. Its optimum temperature is around 82 °F (28 °C), but it stays quite active once water temperature has reached 64–68 °F (18–20 °C). It also appears to react more to abrupt temperature changes than to the actual temperature. Those who set out to catch it, very quickly realize that a shift from 61 to 64 °F (from 16 to 18 °C) is preferable to one from 72 to 68 °F (from 22 to 20 °C), but that, overall, 70 °F (21 °C) should be more favorable than 64 °F (18 °C). What the catfish likes are improvements in climatic conditions, rather than deteriorations.

The wels catfish tends to be a typical inhabitant of lakes or deep rivers with sandy or silty bottoms abounding with obstacles (water plants, riprap, submerged trees and the submerged remains of human dwellings).

At some times — especially during spawning — it may hunt in the current, just like a salmon. That is so in Spain, especially in the River Segre, upstream from Mequinenza. The development of some catfish populations may also be explained by accelerated eutrophication. Still in

Biology

The jaws of the wels catfish are armed with an array of very small rasping teeth.

Spain, on the Ebro, toward Caspe, the species was not very widespread only a few years ago. Today, there is a population explosion as the water becomes more turbid, on account of the pollution caused by mankind.

Diet

The wels catfish is astonishingly eclectic in its diet. Although its staple prey are herbivorous and omnivorous coarse fish (including barbel, chub, and tench), it varies its diet by hunting after nightfall for schools of bleak at the surface, and taking a duckling, or an aquatic rodent. It is also very fond of crayfish, leeches, and worms.

Sexual maturity is reached at five or six years of age, when, depending on the environment, length is around 3–4½ feet (0.90–1.40 m), and weight 9 to 45 pounds (8–20 kg). Spawning is triggered by the temperature, which must reach a minimum of 68 °F (20 °C). The fish spawn in separate couples, in relatively shallow, weedy water, in which the male constructs a kind of nest. Females are highly prolific; each lays about 9,100 eggs per pound of body weight (20,000/kg). The eggs, which are sticky, are 1/20th of an inch (1.5 mm) in diameter, and take about ten days to incubate. Throughout that time, the male jealously guards the eggs, unceremoniously seeing off all intruders. All wariness is lost, and the male becomes an easy prey for the angler.

Reproduction

The success of spawning depends on many, sometimes random, factors. First and foremost is water temperature, which should never fall below 68 °F (20 °C) for at least three days. Next, the alevins fall victim to many predators (pike, pike-perch, and even their own parents). On reaching an age of two to three months, all those that have survived are themselves attacking alevins.

The very poor sight of the wels catfish, admittedly compensated by many other morphological and physiological attributes, proves that the fish lives in the shadows. During the day, it hunts in fairly shallow water, with peak feeding activity at night, or in the twilight, at which times it may venture into the current, or come close to the surface in reservoir lakes. It is also especially active when the water is stirred up by torrential rain. While it is thought to be generally a solitary fish, more than ten fish of one size may sometimes be found in deep holes. Because of its sensitivity to cold water, the catfish is less active during the winter months.

When lying in ambush, or when resting, the wels catfish has a preference for bottoms cluttered with obstacles.

Fishing techniques

An opportunistic predator, as regards its diet, the wels catfish can be fished from a fixed station, using a live bait, or by means of the itinerant techniques of spinning.

The wels catfish has been fished for centuries in central Europe, where it is prized for its flesh. Hitherto, the species was caught there mainly by netting. The spread of the catfish throughout Europe immediately created real competition between sports anglers, who took this new opportunity by refining, and even inventing, techniques perfectly adapted to catching the predator. It should be noted, all the same, that the catfish lure — the well-known clonck — comes from eastern Europe.

CASTING LURES
This technique, little used for some curious reason, is responsible for many catches, and is especially effective from May to early July. Why, one may ask, should it be otherwise, given that the fish has highly sophisticated vibration receptors, and that, being curious by nature, it does not hesitate to rise up from the bottom towards an interesting sound, as has been shown many times by the clonck.

Lures
Most lures suitable for catching large freshwater or marine predators (bass, pollack) may do. They range in length from 4–6 inches (10–15 cm), and weigh ¾–3 oz/20–90 g. We do not prefer revolving lures for fishing deep holes, although it may make the difference in the summer when the fish hunt near the surface or right in the current, in water at 72–75 °F (22–24 °C).

Where the wels catfish lies, depending on season and time of day

The fish hunts near the banks or just below the surface, mainly at night, or in twilight.

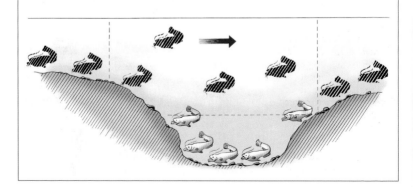

This large wels catfish was caught by spinning, using a wobbling spoon.

One lure of interest is the Mepps Aglia long, no. 5, willow leaf, with a scaly blade. The yellow or orange fluo Giant Killer is also effective, especially in clear weather.

Spoons with two blades are also excellent, or Blue Fox Super Vibrax no. 6, colored or silver, fitted with the vibrating clapper that emits

sounds very audible over a long distance. Lastly, one ought not to overlook the

deadly mixed lures, in which a revolving spoon blade is coupled with a large flexible lure of the shad type.

Revolving spoons usually take more fish. The 2½-oz (70-g) Mepps S, the hook of which is covered by a flexible lure, has proved itself deadly.

Other good models include the 3-ounce (90-g) Yann spoon, whose profile shape enables it to be cast for more than 100 yards (100 m) without much difficulty, the 1-ounce (30-g) Eira, the Toby of the same weight, and the Rapala Inkoo.

Large sizes of flexible lures of shad type, and deep-diving swimming-fish lures must also be included in the fisherman's lure box.

One final point on spoons: in view of the strength of the adversary, the triple

Fishing an excellent current with a flexible lure, on the Rio Cinco (Spain).

Fishing techniques

hooks must be replaced by strengthened models, such as the Gamaktsu no. 59475, or Browning triples, reference 481 4 100 or 481 4 200. A strong casting rod, 10–12½ feet (3–3.5 m) long, specifically intended for catfish, should be chosen, along with a reel with an absolutely reliable ratchet, and 800 feet (250 m) of .4-mm diameter line.

Fishing action
One may fish from the bank or on a boat. When in a boat, care should be taken to avoid any strange noise, such as dropping the rod, or tapping the feet on the bottom of the boat. Real spe-

The clonck, a curious wooden instrument from Romania, which the catfish finds irresistible.

cialists carpet the bottom. Caution in approach, and also swift maneuvering are the keys to success. Once a catfish is hooked, it must be pulled in resolutely, as quickly as possible, so as not to alarm others of its kind in the vicinity.

The spoon is recovered slowly, at bottom level, with the rod tip lowered, and at no faster speed than will set the blade rotating.

There are two decisive points in the struggle: to be able to raise the fish off the bottom, and then to master it when it "de-aerates" (i.e. when it voids its air). A great shower of bubbles appears at the surface, and the fish, which suddenly becomes heavier, makes maximum use of that advantage to seek to return to the bottom and to lie flat

there, stubbornly setting its entire weight against the traction. When the catfish is finally exhausted, and brought to the boat, it must be hauled aboard using the Waller-Guff grip, a procedure that involves grasping the fish by the lower jaw, firmly forcing the thumb into the gaping mouth, firmly pressing back the mass of rasping teeth. The other fingers form a vice on the outer edge of the jaw. A heavy work glove is advisable to avoid injury, but the only real risk comes from the lure, when barbs of the hook can be seen outside the mouth. The catfish is then traditionally roped up, to keep it alive to be photographed before it is released.

LIVE BAIT FISHING

This is certainly one of the most often used and most regularly successful techniques when fishing for the largest catfish. The standard procedure, with a floating line, may be used and is rewarding in the spring, when the fish are hunting in fairly shallow water. The basic rig may be the same as that recommended for pike fishing, for example, taking care to use spindle-shaped controller floats, which are far more sensitive and will not make the catfish suspicious when there is a touch, because they offer less resistance to being pulled under the water surface.

Fishing by sight, letting the float drift toward the eddies

A superb catfish, caught by spinning, in the Rhône.

A fine Spanish catfish caught in the village of Mequinenza, the mecca for catfish anglers.

Sliding weight rig.
*Above: basic.
Below: variant for separating the live bait.*

stirred up by the predator, is an exciting technique. A float with a small sail may be very useful for carrying the line along, always providing the wind is blowing in the right direction. The touch is usually distinct, with the fish sucking in its victim, before dragging along the line in its turn.

When the float disappears, wait for a short time before striking broadly and firmly.

Weighted live bait

This technique immobilizes the live bait in a precise place, at depth or in cluttered localities.

Most rigs are developments of the paternoster, and have a cast adjusted to enable the fish to pass over obstacles. Whether it be for fishing with weighted live bait, or with a floating line, the basic equipment is a 10–11-foot (3.3–3.6-m) rod, with a

Livebait rig with buoy

Floating line set to halt the live bait, just below the surface, at the chosen station.

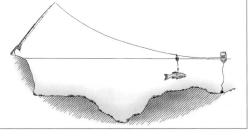

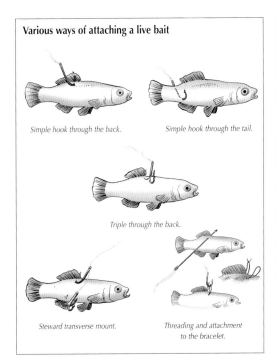

Various ways of attaching a live bait

Simple hook through the back.

Simple hook through the tail.

Triple through the back.

Steward transverse mount.

Threading and attachment to the bracelet.

Floating line rigs

Variant with axial float.

Variant with spinning top float, attached by the quill.

strength of between 3 and 4 pounds (1.4–1.8 kg). The reel should be able to hold 800 feet (250 m) of .50-diameter nylon line. Reels with a fighting brake or a release mechanism to take off the brake in a tenth of a second are very useful, because the first rushes of the catfish are rather spectacular.

Livebait rods, with floating line, for setting in open water.

Keeping a careful watch on floats going under far out in the water. Binoculars are very useful.

Other baits

Being an opportunistic predator, the catfish also likes a good, well-presented bundle of worms, or a cluster of leeches on a simple hook (size 4 or 5). Weighted rigs for this purpose are based on the method used by carp anglers, of off-the-bottom rigs. The bait is rendered more attractive and visible by being raised above the obstacles strewn over the bottom. The trick is to tie a thread carrying a small polystyrene ball (⅗ in./15 cm) on the curve of the hook. A fairly small hook (size 2–6) for the bait is attached to the end of the thread. The length of the leader depends on how cluttered the bottom is. The usual length is between 20–33 inches (50–80 cm).

A teaser placed in front of the weight.

Rig for fishing with the clonck and worms.
Left: compact rig.
Right: flexible rig.

FISHING WITH A MANIPULATED DEAD FISH

This technique is found to be particularly effective when fishing deep holes, at times when the catfish are still lethargic, and not very inclined to dash madly after a spoon or a flexible lure.

The equipment needed is the same as for fishing with lures, but the procedure using very light rigs may be just as

GOOD LIVE BAITS FOR CATFISH

Resistance is the first quality for a good live bait for catfish. It must struggle for as long as possible at the end of the line, so as to give a continuous signal. Such species as carp, tench, and goldfish, which are very active, are therefore specially attractive. The question that always arises is what size of live bait. The catfish sometimes hunts primarily for large fish of 1–2 pounds (500 g–1 kg). On other occasions it gorges on small fish about 4–6 inches (10–15 cm) long, such as roach, gudgeon, and small bream. The attachment of the live bait is very important, because of the lined, very hard, mouth of the catfish. Many specialists prefer simple, strong iron hooks, size 4, for example, which must be very sharp, rather than triples, which have less sharp points, and are capable of seriously injuring the hand when landing the fish. Lastly, a floating line, because the ability of the catfish to come to hunt at the surface, whatever the depth of the locality, should never be underestimated. The line should always be adjusted to keep the live bait at least 6 feet (about 2 m) below the surface. Lastly, it should be noted that the taste and smell of the bait (use of artificial substitutes) remains under-exploited, and would appear to be not without interest, e.g. a carefully mixed ground bait when fishing with an inert dead fish.

Simple strong iron hook.

effective in the summer when fishing currents and shallows. The fish is then worked in a more sustained manner, and flutters like a wobbling spoon. The rig is certainly lighter. It derives, in all respects, more or less from the rigs used when fishing for all predators, but special care should be taken to see that it is very robust. In particular, the hooks should be solid, should not lose their shape, and should be very sharp.

Roping a catfish to the boat: not to be recommended.

WHITEFISH

Biology

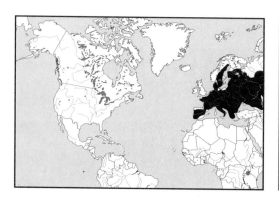

FOREIGN NAMES

French: carpe.
German: Karpfen.
Spanish: carpa.

DESCRIPTION

The carp (*Cyprinus carpio*) is the largest fish in the Cyprinidae family. It may measure up to 3 feet (1 m) in length at a weight approaching 88 pounds (40 kg). Its dorsal fin is long and has a thick, toothed initial spine. The ventral fins are placed behind the pectoral fins and directly beneath the dorsal fin.

The carp has a protractile mouth with fleshy lips. The upper lips have four barbels, the front two short and thin, the other two, at the corners of the mouth, long and thick.

VARIETIES

Essentially, three varieties of carp can be found:

– *The common carp*
The common carp is covered in scales. Its back is greenish or bluish-brown, and the sides are ocher mixed with glints of gray and old gold. The belly is white or otherwise yellowish.

– *The mirror carp*
Has a thickset, slightly humped body. There are large scales on the back, at the base of the fins, at the root of the tail, and near the gill covers. Its skin has purplish blue tones.

– *The leather carp*
Its thick, weathered skin resembles leather, hence the name. The belly is yel-

The common carp is recognizable by its scaly body.

With its thick, weathered skin, the leather carp is well-named.

lowish and the body is more humped than that of the mirror carp.

BEHAVIOR

The carp breeds between May and July. The females reach sexual maturity between the ages of three and four years and the males at two years. Accompanied by noisy flurries, spawning takes place at temperatures of at least 68 °F (20 °C). At lower temperatures spawning is delayed. Carp spawn in shallow water and the female sheds her eggs on plants, roots, or logs. The carp has always been the subject of claims and theories surrounded by mystery. Basically gregarious, carp move about in fairly large shoals, but become more solitary as the years pass. They feed on the bottom using the barbels on the mouth as tactile organs. Despite their reputation as herbivores, carp mainly feed on chironomid larvae (bloodworms). The vegetable plankton that they consume represents, however, less than ten percent of their diet. Their feeding rhythm slows when the temperature drops.

Carp prefer to live in slow-moving waters which warm up very quickly and where the current is weak. Known carp haunts are ponds, reservoirs and gravel pits, but this majestic cyprinoid colonizes medium-sized and large rivers in particular. Here heavy specimens are often caught.

The mirror carp is distinguished from the other species by its squat, slightly humped body.

Fishing techniques

Carp fishing techniques have been modernized over the years. If the methods used by our forebears are still effective, legering and pole fishing are highly rated for the thrills they provide.

ROD FISHING

This method has developed strongly with the creation of artificial lakes dedicated specially to carp fishing. Highly prized in Italy and Great Britain and most often privately owned, these stretches of water enable fishermen to capture heavy fish on fine, light tackle.

Tackle
– The rod
For this very special kind of fish, all the makers have created "carp and big fish" rods for inclusion in their ranges. These special carbon rods measure between 30 and 40 feet (10–13 m). They are equipped with a very short hollow tip from which exits the elastic of large diameter (.04 to .06 in. [1–1.6 mm]), and it passes through two or three sections, giving enough reserve to allow the landing of hard-fighting fish.

– The line and rig
The diameter of the line is between .18 mm and .20 mm at least.

A stubby float with a long antenna in balsa or bamboo is attached to this line. With an antenna of this type the float does not drift when bulky baits are used.
The weight consists of shot bunched together or combined with an olivette. The hook is solid, round and varies in size between 10 and 18 according to whichever bait is in use.

Groundbaiting
In lakes, vegetable (grain) or living bait are just as effective as is groundbait. In medium-sized or large rivers a heavy, filling groundbait is more suitable. Commercial, ready-to-use "carp and big fish" groundbait saves time and avoids

A special "big fish" rod is essential for handling carp of several pounds.

CARP *(Cyprinus carpio)*

The maggot is a bait much appreciated by fine carp.
It is used both as bait and groundbait.

mistakes. In preparing groundbait for carp, do not hesitate to use filling, fatty, sticky materials. On the other hand, carp are fond of all kinds of cake, flours, and semolinas derived from maize grain. Coarse white breadcrumbs, maize semolina, seedcake, milled linseed, milled hempseed, oily peanuts, biscuit, and soya flour comprise the materials currently in use.

Baits

– The bloodworm
Despite its fragility and small size, the bloodworm is much liked by heavy fish. A bunch of several worms on a 14 or a 16 hook is best.

– The maggot
Much loved by large fish, the maggot is a standard bait that can also serve as groundbait. The large white or (red or yellow) colored gozzer is preferable.

– Maize
Maize is an essential carp fishing bait. Clean and inexpensive, it is easily obtained in retail outlets. It is used in its natural state but is also available in dyed or flavored varieties (vanilla, strawberry, tutti frutti, etc.). Maize is used both on the hook and for regular groundbaiting. The maize grain is put on a 14 to 16 hook. For the effective capture of larger fish, two grains can be used on a size 10 to 12 hook.

– Cooked hempseed
Cooked hempseed, mostly used to tempt the roach, is also much appreciated by carp. However, because of its small size, it is not much used.

– Mini-boilies
Boilies are too bulky (see under boilies in the next chapter) to be used with a floating line. On the other hand, a small boilie a few millimeters in diameter, hair-mounted or stuck on (see mounting in the next chapter) is particularly effective.

Fishing action
Before pole fishing for carp, a good location has to be chosen. In open water carp betray their presence by repeated jumps and characteristic swirls.
The presence of plants, old logs or dead trees nearby is a good sign. Carp will seek refuge among these snags.

Two or three rods are standard equipment for legering.

Once the spot has been chosen, groundbaiting must be carried out. If the site is not frequented too much by other fishermen, it is advisable to groundbait for several days in advance.

Maize grain is best for groundbaiting in open water. The amount to be used depends on the concentration of fish present. However 4 to 6 pounds (2–3 kg) of maize are enough for a day's fishing. The maize is scattered by hand or with a catapult with light elastic. When the location has been plumbed, the line is carefully adjusted so that the cast rests on the bottom.

The carp will reach the groundbait only slowly unless plenty of fish are present. The bite is characteristic. The float sinks deep, or just the opposite, rises on the surface. Given the action of the rod, there is no point in striking. Once hooked, the carp makes no flourishes. It plows straight ahead. It's at this point that the size and strength of the elastic can be fully justified. The rod is slanted in the opposite direction to that taken by the fish, which always tries to snag the line and break it.

When the carp begins to show signs of fatigue, simply unjoint the rod slowly, keeping the line taut and in contact with the fish. The landing net is lowered quietly into the water to avoid alarming the fish. Even at the last moment the carp may make a desperate rush in an attempt to escape.

Once the fish is inside the ring of the net, the rod is placed on the rod rest and it is hoisted toward the bank using both hands. The carp is unhooked carefully and slipped into a large, deep keepnet.

A fine carp that succumbed to this deadly technique.

Rod battery

Rod rests, bite detectors and audible bite alarms go to make up the well-organized carp fisherman's rod battery.

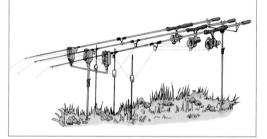

LEGERING

The arrival of this technique from Great Britain revolutionized traditional European fishing methods and was followed by a radical upheaval of tackle, attitudes, and ethics. All carp fishermen worthy of the name practice "catch and release" policy, and every carp is returned to the water with the greatest of care. Modern legering calls for an imposing array of tackle, sometimes at the top of the range, for the capture of trophy fish. Once the craze was over, the lure of tackle and high technology was to serve the carp-fisherman ill: he became somewhat marginalized. Today, thanks to contributions that have been made by some of the great names in carp fishing, by

the media and through competitions, legering has regained its drive and dynamism and is now more acceptable to the more traditional fishermen.

Tackle

– Rods

These are of carbon or Kevlar, are in two sections and between 11½ to 12½ feet (3.60–3.90 m) in length. The power and solidity of these rods make it possible to cast heavy weights 2½ to 3 ounces (80–100 g) long dis-

tances without difficulty. Commercially available rods are rated in pounds. Their power ranges from 1½ to 4 pounds, in steps of a quarter or a half-pound.

– Reelt

This essential item must be chosen with care: well-balanced, with a perfectly sized tough roller and equipped with an efficient drag system (rear or front, for use while playing the fish or not), capable of giving or taking line at great speed. The spool capacity is from 800 to 1000 feet (250–300 m).

– The line

The line is of nylon or braid. A .35 mm line with a breaking strength of 15 to 24 pounds (7 –11 kg) is standard. Good quality fluorescent nylon is an advantage in detecting movement of the line at a glance. Braid is mostly used for the cast. However, it can also be used to fill the reel. It is supple and stronger than monofilament nylon at a smaller diameter. As it is not very elastic and has no memory, its

Bite indicators, or "squirrels," detect the smallest line movement.

Fishing techniques

No carp leger fisherman can ignore the boilie as a bait

great strength can also be a disadvantage, especially when hooking a fish.

The weight of the lead clearly depends on the power of the rod. There are five basic types of lead in use: the Arlesey bomb, the missile, the Stealth, the triple-lobed and the bullet. The hook, the final link in the chain, is chosen by its shape and type of point. Its strength is also very important. An inturned point and a short shank are used for baits resting on the bottom. For floating baits it is better to use long-shanked hooks with straight points. A number of small accessories are equally important in the preparation of the rig.

A swivel is used to attach the line to the cast. Fixed or sliding anti-tangle tubing stiffens the end section and prevents the cast from twisting round the line. Soluble line known as PVA has the capacity of dissolving in the water and freeing bait on the bottom. Round, oval, hard or tulip-shaped beads serve as stops or shock absorbers to protect the attachment knot. Double beads are used to fix legers and floats in certain rigs.

– Accessories

Modern carp fishing calls for a certain number of essential accessories:

• A rod rest or rod pod, allowing several rods to be controlled at the same time.

• A bite indicator, known as a "squirrel", which allows the least movement of the line to be detected.

• An audible bite alarm that sounds when a fish is moving off and which emits a loud, shrill signal.

• A large landing net, 6 – 6½ feet (1.8–2 m) in length, with an opening at least 3 feet (1 m) wide.

• An umbrella and folding bed are two essential items. The first gives protection against cold, sun, rain, and wind. The folding bed (or chair-bed) provides somewhere comfortable on which to wait for bites when conditions are good. It will be found to be indispensable for night fishing.

Baits

– The boilie

This is the standard carp fisherman's bait. It is a ball of colored paste aromatized and rich in protein. Most carp fishermen make their own boilies starting with a protein-rich base to which they add their own preferred colors and aromas. There are also commercially produced, ready-to-use boilies for those who are not inclined to cook, or lack the necessary time. Boilies range in size from ½ inch to 1 inch (14–24 mm). The ½ inch (14 mm) boilies are primarily intended for groundbaiting. The .6, .7 and .78 inch (16, 18 and 20 mm) boilies are used in classic fishing. The 1 inch (24 mm) boilies are for big carp and for groundbaiting at great distances. Boilies are attached by a procedure known as hair baiting. This is the result of close observation of the way in which carp feed. The principle is simple: separate the bait from the hook. The hair is a very short piece of nylon, Dacron or braid attached to the eye or to the very short shank of the hook. This small length has a loop onto which the boilie is threaded using a baiting needle. When the carp sucks in the boilie, the hook follows. The carp swallows the bait but its mouth is then pierced by the hook.

– Particle baits
In addition to boilies, various grains are effective baits for fine carp.
• Maize
Hair-rigged as for boilies, on a size 4 hook, maize continues to be a standard particle bait for carp fishing. The more fragile sweetcorn can also be used mounted four

or five grains on a hair, with a size 4 to 6 hook.
• Hempseed
Hempseed may be used with a size 4 or 6 hook, threading a few seeds on a hair with a sewing needle.
• Broad bean
After soaking in water for 48 hours to plump it up, the bean is fixed on a hair, with a size 6 hook.
• Yellow or white lupin
The lupin (the seed of a plant in the pea family) is also used on a hair, armed with a size 4 to 6 hook.
• Tiger nut

Troublesome and not much used, it must be soaked for at least 24 hours before use.
• Peanut
Rich in oil, needs soaking, used at medium distances on a size 4 to 6 hook.

Groundbaiting
Groundbaiting is always carried out at a distance from the bank. Carp fishermen often use a boat or small radio-controlled boat that has been specifically devised for the purpose.
For groundbaiting from the bank, a catapult or a groundbaiting tube, called a cobra, must be used.
This instrument is much used by carp fishermen. It

Netting the fish, crucial and exciting.

Fishing techniques

This carp was caught on hair-mounted maize.

makes it possible to throw boilies a distance of 50–70 feet (16–20 m) up to 300 feet (100 m) from the bank. The quantity of grain or boilies allocated to ground-baiting depends on the density of fish and the extent of the fishing location. In a stretch of water containing many carp, 18–22 pounds (8–10 kg) of grain and about 1,000 boilies would suffice for groundbait.

Fishing action

With groundbaiting complete, the line must be cast. The cast is made overhead, one hand on the rod butt and the other on the upper handle with the index finger holding the line.

The line hangs down behind, just above the ground. The action of the rod is then used to give impetus to the line in the appropriate direction. When the weight is on the bottom in the groundbaited

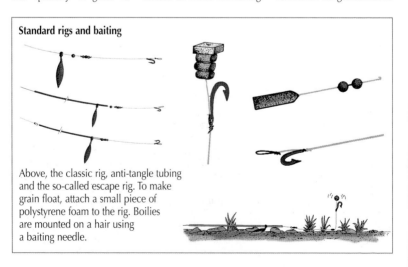

Standard rigs and baiting

Above, the classic rig, anti-tangle tubing and the so-called escape rig. To make grain float, attach a small piece of polystyrene foam to the rig. Boilies are mounted on a hair using a baiting needle.

Essential movements

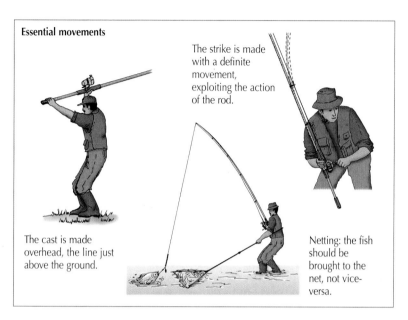

The strike is made with a definite movement, exploiting the action of the rod.

The cast is made overhead, the line just above the ground.

Netting: the fish should be brought to the net, not vice-versa.

area, the bale arm is closed and the line tightened to remove the slack. The rod is placed on the rest with the drag set neither too tight nor too loose.

The line is placed in the bite indicator, in the upper third of the metal shaft. Finally the audible bite alarm is switched on. The bite is the best moment in carp fishing. The bite indicator rises to the top of the shaft releasing the line and setting off the detector alarm.

The strike is made without violence, but with enough motion to embed the hook in the fish's throat. At first the carp tries to make off by taking line. The fight, often prolonged, consists of recovering line while adjusting the drag with the free hand. When the carp begins to tire, it is led gently toward the landing net which should already be in position. The fish is brought to the net, not vice-versa. One must always be ready to release

the drag quickly, since when the carp sees the net it struggles and makes a final leap, always finding enough strength to try and escape. Once the fish is in the net, this is taken in both hands and brought back to the bank. To unhook the carp some sort of receiving pad is essential: this avoids injury to the fish and gives the fisherman a perfect background against which he can then admire it and take photographs under the best possible conditions.

Biology

DESCRIPTION

The bream, of the Cyprinidae family, is recognized by its deep flat body. Two species are distinguished: the white, or silver bream (*Blicca bjoerkna*) and the great, or common bream (*Abramis brama*). The white bream is nicknamed "plate" or "little plate". The bream has ventral fins located behind the pectoral fins but forward of the dorsal fin. The tail fin is deeply indented. The mouth is bare with protractile lips. The sides are covered in scales, its back olive-green or brown, the body light gray tinged with pink, blue, or gold in large bream, the belly white.

The size of bream varies from 1 to 1½ feet (30–50 cm) up to 2¼ feet (70 cm) at a weight that may reach more than 6½ pounds (3 kg). The bream's body is covered in abundant sticky mucus that has earned it the name of "dribbler". This adhesive mucus sticks to the cast, the landing net, the keep net, and the angler's clothes.

GEOGRAPHIC DISTRIBUTION

The bream is very prolific in much of central and also northwest Europe. It is, how-ever, unfortunately absent from the Iberian peninsula.

The white bream is also nicknamed "plate" or "little plate".

The great bream is prolific; it lives mostly on the bottom.

BEHAVIOR

The bream easily produces hybrids with the roach. These hybrid fish are encountered in large streams and especially in rivers. The bream breeds in May–June. As with the roach, the males acquire nuptial livery and are covered in small buttons that make the body rough.

The female bream lays up to 300,000 eggs on weeds in the shallows. The bream is resistant to pollution and may be present in both still and running water.

Its constant increase is explained by the retreat of large predators such as the pike, but the massive influx of catfish in the waterways may stem this proliferation in the future. The bream likes to live in ponds, tanks, wet docks, canals, slow rivers, and reservoirs. It is very numerous in rivers, where it reaches a considerable size. The bream is a gregarious bottom feeder that eats bloodworms, plankton, crustaceans, and mollusks. Its method of feeding is characteristic, moving from side to side, head down. Much sought by match fishermen as a favorite catch, the often-ignored bream can prove as fickle as a roach or a bleak. When bream are biting, a bag of some tens of kilos may be easily taken.

Fishing techniques

The bream is abundant in medium-sized and large rivers, canals, lakes, and ponds. All rod-fishing techniques can be used with success.

ROD FISHING
Tackle
– The rod

A carbon rod identical to that used for roach is perfectly suitable. It has a hollow tip with an elastic threaded through two or three sections.

– The line

The set-up of the line depends on the fish sought and the place chosen. For bream fishing in canals or ponds, line .8 mm to .10 mm in diameter will be found to be adequate. The float, carrot- or spindle-shaped, weighs from .3 to 1.2 g. It is balanced with a

bunch of shot or an olivette combined with shot.

For stream and river fishing, it is preferable to choose a thicker line – between .12 mm and .14 mm. A larger float is also used, ball- or pear-shaped, provided with a long antenna and stem to give good stability. The hook will be chosen according to the bait used. Most recommended is the round type in sizes from 10 to about 18.

Groundbaiting

The bream is a cyprinid that loves groundbait. It is equally content with bait, whether living or vegetable. Groundbait for bream is filling and fatty, sticky, and heavy when used in the current. Breadcrumbs, biscuit, peanuts, all maize derivatives (gluten, seedcake, semolina) are first-class ingredients.

The pole is very effective for large bream.

Baits

The classic roach baits also do well for bream. Bloodworm, maggots and wheat are very effective. Brandlings are also much liked by large bream and will often make all the difference when the fish are sulking.

Fishing action

When the location has been carefully plumbed, groundbaiting is carried out. This will be considerable, consisting of a dozen orange-sized balls stuffed with bait. When the bream arrive on the spot, they give away their presence by fine bubbles. Since bream like static bait, it is advisable to throw in more balls of groundbait – one for each cast of the line – which will sink to the bottom. When the bait is taken, the bite is characteristic. The float rises and lies flat on the water. A light strike will ensure that the fish is hooked.

REEL FISHING

Methods vary according to the location one is trying. Float fishing is effective in slow rivers, in ponds and canals. Legering is preferable in large rivers and reservoirs. Bolognese technique fishing is only used in rivers with a strong current and when the wind is favorable (blowing upstream).

Float fishing
The tackle and fishing method are identical to those used for roach.

With reel fishing, or when far from the bank, a catapult is used for groundbaiting.

Legering
The rod used is made from carbon and measures between 10 to 13 feet (3.0–3.9 m). It is equipped with a long, sensitive bite indicator (quiver) at the tip. The line from the reel is .14 mm or .16 mm and fitted with a feeder filled with groundbait or bait, or both, to provide for continuous on-the-spot delivery.

Fishing action
When the hook is baited, the feeder is loaded with a handful of groundbait. The line is then cast in the chosen spot. With the line in place, the pick-up arm is closed to sink the line. In calm water, the rod is positioned parallel to the bank with the line and the tip at right angles. In streams and rivers the rod is placed vertically on a long spike driven into the ground so as to resist the current. The bite of the bream on the bait is

unmistakable. The quiver tip either bends or slackens completely. The strike is made horizontally sideways, with a firm action.

THE BOLOGNESE TECHNIQUE
Long used by Italian fishermen, the Bolognese method gives excellent results when fishing for bream in a constant current.

Tackle
The rod is carbon, telescopic and fitted with raised rings. Its length varies from 15 to 23 feet (5 to 7 m). A classic reel as used in float fishing completes the basic tackle. The line is .12 mm to .18 mm line with a squat float capable of carrying a good weight. The antenna is bulky and made of plastic, balsa, or bamboo. The weight consists of two large spherical leads. A size 10 to 18 hook is mounted on a section of line that is about

15 inches (40 cm) long and is attached to the main line by a small swivel.

Fishing action
In the so-called Bolognese fishing technique, the line is drifted downstream. Groundbait should be thrown opposite, or even slightly downstream, rather than too far upstream. The rod is kept high, held against the groin. When there is a bite, the float sinks deep in the current. To hook the fish, the fisherman pulls the rod toward himself using the forearm.

TENCH (TINCA TINCA)

The tench is a cyprinid that loves weed.

BIOLOGY

Description
The tench (*Tinca tinca*) is one of the most beautiful fishes in the cyprinid family. Its body is squat, rounded and covered in small scales and thick mucus. It is a greenish-brown color, or a bluish-brown on the back. The sides are green with hints of yellow gold, the belly white or yellow. The tench's mouth is protractile and has two short barbels at the angles. At 2 feet (60 cm) it may reach a weight of 11 pounds (5 kg).

Geographical distribution
Present in the greater part of Europe, the tench becomes inactive when the water temperature falls below 50 °F (10 °C).

Behavior
The tench breeds between May and July depending on the water temperature. A bottom feeder, it loves weed. It is found mainly in ponds, canals and slow rivers overgrown by water lilies, duckweed and other vegetation. It feeds on bloodworms, caddis larvae, and mollusks.

FISHING TECHNIQUES

Legering
Tench can normally be taken with a traditional fishing rod. For large specimens legering is the most suitable method.

Tackle
– The rod
A "quiver" or "feeder" rod in carbon between 10½ and 12½ feet (3.30 and 3.90 m) in length is perfectly suitable. This is equipped with bite indicators of different sensitivities.

With its green sides and yellow-gold reflections, the tench is not difficult to recognize.

– The reel
A classic skirted or fixed-spool reel, wound with .14 mm to .20 mm line up to the lip of the spool makes up the basic tackle.
– The line
The rig is similar to that used for bream. An Arlesey bomb and a feeder are added, or either a clip swivel or a very short piece of Power gum. The feeder is mostly used in lakes or rivers. In shallow ponds it is best to use an Arlesey bomb.

Groundbaiting and baits

Tench are susceptible to groundbait. A brown, sugary granular mixture is preferable. Breadcrumbs, treacly copra, maize seedcake or maize semolina are standard ingredients. Tench have a weakness for gingerbread, powdered, or if the commercial product in blocks is used, scalded. The most effective baits for tench are maggots, bunches of bloodworm or brandlings. Sweetcorn may be added, as may wheat, in balls of groundbait. Boilies are equally attractive but they should be small, preferably sweetened, and colored orange or yellow.

Fishing action

Pond fishing is the most productive. A long corridor between water lilies is an ideal spot in which to catch this attractive cyprinid. Once the cast is made, the rod is placed on a rest parallel to the bank with the bite indicator exactly level with the water. A bite is indicated by a slight bending of the indicator. The strike is a strong movement, pulling the rod back. The tench puts up a strong and ferocious defense. It turns in big swirls on the spot or moves deliberately toward the bank where the fisherman is. Caution is recommended in bringing it to the net.

The capture of a tench is always a happy moment for the fisherman.

Biology

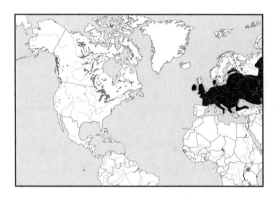

FOREIGN NAMES

French: rotengle.
German: Rotfeder,
Röttel.
Italian: scardola.

DESCRIPTION

The rudd (*Scardinius ery-throphthalmus*) belongs to the cyprinid family and is one of its most attractive members. It is often confused with the roach. However, the roach is distinguished by its flatter, more convex body. The rudd's back is greenish with reddish tinges and its sides and belly silver with pinkish-gold or red reflections. The fins are scarlet and the eyes ringed with gold. The ventral fins are attached decidedly forward of the dorsal fin which finishes directly above the start of the anal fin. The bare nose is distinctly upturned. Size varies from 4 to 8 inches (10–20 cm) for weights of ½ and 3 ounces (15–100 g). However, large rudd of over a couple of pounds are often caught.

GEOGRAPHIC DISTRIBUTION

The rudd is distributed throughout central Europe. Different varieties exist, particularly in Italian waters, where it is called the "scardola".

BEHAVIOR

The rudd lays up to 100,000 eggs which become attached to aquatic plants. Spawning takes place from April to May in still water, ponds, slow rivers, and canals that are rich in vegetation.

Unlike the roach, the rudd is fond of the surface. It likes to live anywhere rich in vegetation, mainly in ponds.

Primarily gregarious, the rudd feeds at the surface of the water. Its food consists of aquatic insects, larvae, and plant debris.

With its scarlet fins, the rudd is one of the prettiest cyprinids.

RUDD *(Scardinius erythrophthalmus)*

A fine rudd taken on rod and reel.

Fishing techniques

The rudd is essentially a surface fish, which limits the methods used to fish for it. Pole fishing and float fishing with rod and reel are the two methods used.

ROD FISHING

The rudd is fished for in the same way as for the roach. A carbon rod is recommended: the length varies according to the fishing location.

Tackle

Lines and rigs

Fishing for rudd is even more subtle and delicate than for roach. Fine, supple line between .6 mm and .10 mm is perfectly suitable. For very large rudd a greater diameter is advisable – between .10 mm and .12 mm. The float must be sensitive, ball- or pear-shaped, with a short quill, and balanced with bunched split shot. The hook should be fine, "crystal" shape and appropriate to whatever bait is used.

Groundbaiting

A commercial mixture composed of half pond and half surface groundbait is ideal. The rudd is sensitive to color and to groundbait that forms a fine cloud. Yellow, orange, and white seem to be the best-liked colors. A mixture may be improved by adding a trace of the chosen color.

Baits

The bloodworm and the maggot are the best known for taking good rudd. Bread and paste may also be added to these.

In the summer rudd will not refuse a small green grasshopper, a fly, or a cunningly presented caterpillar.

Fishing action

Before fishing for rudd, it is as well to choose a spot where there is plenty of vegetation. Banks of reed and water lilies close by are an added asset. The rudd betrays its presence by small rings close to the plants; it may even momentarily leave the water for a lily leaf before slipping back. The groundbait is moistened so that it breaks up quietly at the surface forming a good cloud. A pinch of bloodworm or some pinkies will make the preparation more attractive. At the same time, one can

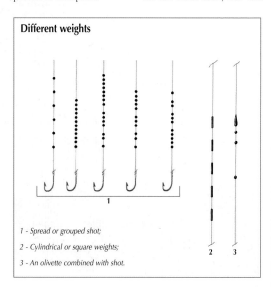

Different weights

1 - Spread or grouped shot;

2 - Cylindrical or square weights;

3 - An olivette combined with shot.

keep groundbaiting the spot by throwing in some mixed bait by itself, using a small catapult with very light elastic. The line is controlled so that the bait moves at the surface or in mid-water. The bite of the rudd is characteristic: the float rises and moves slightly sideways before plunging deep into the water.

Rudd may attain several pounds.

A fine rudd in its golden livery.

HOTU *(CHONDROSTOMA NASUS)*

BIOLOGY

Description
The hotu (*Chondrostoma nasus*) is a cyprinid with a streamlined body, originating in central Europe, particularly from the Danube basin. It has a broad snout and a bare mouth. The ventral fins are located behind the pectoral fins at the level of the dorsal fin. The hotu breeds between March and May.

Geographic distribution
The hotu is spread throughout eastern Europe. It is also found on the Iberian peninsula. These "southern" hotu, smaller in size, are particularly combative and fickle.

Behavior
The female lays about 50,000 to 100,000 eggs on a gravel or shingle bed. Basically gregarious, the hotu, like the barbel, likes spring waters, and is also found in large rivers. It has long been considered by fishermen to be the cause of considerable damage: it is accused of attacking alevins and the eggs of other species, though no evidence has been discovered to support this reputation. In fact the hotu feeds on worms, larvae, crustaceans, and mosses or aquatic plants.

FISHING TECHNIQUES

Rod fishing
Tackle
– The rod
A carbon rod as used in fishing for other cyprinids is standard equipment. It is important however to make sure it is sufficiently rigid and strong, especially for river fishing. The rod has a hollow tip with a medium to large elastic through it.

The hotu has a streamlined body with a broad snout and bare mouth.

Rod and reel fishing, especially by the Bolognese method, is best for hotu.

– The line

The line is strong, consisting of .12 mm to .16 line, with a squat float with a plastic, bamboo or glass fiber antenna. The weight of the float is chosen in keeping with the current and depth at the selected spot. The float is weighted with a group of split shot or an olivette combined with shot. The hook is round, from size 10 to 18.

Goundbaiting and baits

The hotu is partial to bread-based groundbaits. Coarse white or brown breadcrumbs make up the base of the preparation, and the composition may include such ingredients as pumpkin flour, ground walnut, milled linseed, or poppy seed. Otherwise, a commercial groundbait for large fish is just as effective. This groundbait is enriched (especially in the current) by the addition of live or even frozen baits such as maggots or casters. Baits attractive to hotu are white or colored (red, bronze, or yellow) maggots, bloodworm, brandlings, wheat or maize grain, bread, or a small cube of cooked potato.

Fishing action

Fishing for hotu is most productive in medium and large rivers. After plumbing carefully, a dozen orange-sized balls of groundbait are used. The line is controlled so that the bait just brushes the bottom. The bite of the hotu is fast and heavy. The strike should be sustained, especially if there is a current. In fact, the hotu has a small, very hard mouth penetrated only with some difficulty by the hook. The hotu puts up a lively defense and the landing net should be used every time. If a shoal of fish is about, it is possible to make a bag of several pounds.

Biology

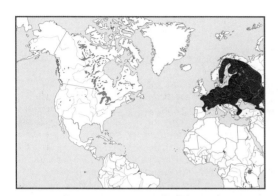

FOREIGN NAMES

French: *gardon*.
German: *Plötze*, *Rotauge*.
Spanish: *gobio*.

With its silvery-blue sides, the roach is the bank-fisherman's preferred fish.

ROACH *(Rutilus rutilus)*

As seen in this photo, the position of the roach's mouth shows it is a ready bottom feeder

DESCRIPTION

The roach (*Rutilus rutilus*) is a member of the cyprinid family and, indisputably, is one of the most popular whitefish found in the Northern Hemisphere.

It is the bank fisherman's favorite. The roach is recognized by its streamlined shape. Its sides are silvery, slightly bluish, its fins and eyes orange. The mouth is bare, at the end of a slightly upturned snout. The size of roach varies from 6 to 12 inches (15–30 cm) at a weight going from ⅓ ounce (10 g) to an average 10 ounces (500 gm). Some large specimens may reach 16 or 20 inches (40–50 cm) and weigh 2 to 4 pounds (1–2 kg). Sexual maturity is reached toward the age of two or three years. Spawning takes place in April or June, depending on the region and the water temperature. The roach gather in shallow water. The males assume their nuptial attire – the head and back become covered in small white buttons and the skin becomes very rough. Females in the same shoal spawn at the same time. They lay about 100,000 eggs that stick to the aquatic vegetation.

GEOGRAPHIC DISTRIBUTION

The roach is extensively distributed in central Europe, except for Spain, Italy and some parts of the Scandinavian countries. Apart from some high altitude rivers, the roach can be found in ponds, reservoirs, wet docks, slow rivers, streams, and canals. In certain northern European countries enormous concentrations of large roach are seen at the start of the spring (the end of April until the beginning of May). This phenomenon also occurs in Sweden's southern rivers (the Sege and the Lodde).

BEHAVIOR

The roach likes sandy bottoms and mud, overgrown with weeds. It is generally gregarious, but the larger fish are more solitary. The roach's food consists of mollusks, and it also likes midge (chironome) larvae (the bloodworm used by bank fishermen) and trichoptera (phyriganeids). In summer, the roach eats large quantities of planktonic algae. Adult roach are also attracted by zooplankton. Roach seek their food mainly on the bottom, though they may also position themselves in midwater from time to time.

This adult roach is easily identifiable by its sturdy outline and rounded shape.

Fishing techniques

The roach is a suspicious, fickle fish. It calls for techniques with a great deal of finesse. Pole- and float-fishing with rod and reel are the most effective.

ROD FISHING
Tackle
– The rod
Nowadays the most commonly used material is carbon, sometimes combined with Kevlar, boron or liquid crystal.

Two types of rod can be mentioned: telescopic and sectional rods that can be broken down. Telescopic rods are liked because they are easily collapsed and occupy little space. They are suitable for fishing close

to the bank or from a boat. They have a soft action and the ideal length varies between 9 and 18 feet (3 and 6 m).

Sectional rods are more often used. They are rigid and light, and their length can be altered as needed. They can reach great lengths, as long as 44 feet (14.5 m). For roach, a rod of 30 or 35 feet (10 or 11 m) will do very well. This enables the use of a line shorter than the rod. The rod

Baiting

Through the head, the most common method.

Through the middle, when the roach are not really biting.

Match fishermen are reputed to know all the secrets of roach fishing.

Much attention is given to groundbait for roach. It should be dark and moderately fine.

plastics are the most commonly used.

The float is balanced so as to sink to antenna level or even lower, with split shot, cylindrical leads, or an olivette combined with shot.

The weights vary according to the fishing location, the speed of the current, the depth, and the force of the wind. When the roach are biting, a large weight is fixed near the hook. Otherwise it is preferable to spread the weights out or move them closer to the float, so as to allow the line a gentler descent.

Hooks used for roach are fine, "crystal" shape or round and somewhat stronger. The size is from No.12 to No.24 depending on the bait used. The cast, from 6 to 9 inches (15–20 cm) long, is one- or two-hundredths smaller in diameter than the line, to which it is joined loop-to-loop.

can be shortened as necessary. It has a hollow top section through which passes an elastic. This ingenious arrangement serves to avoid breakage by a big fish when using the very fine line needed to overcome the roach's natural suspicion.

– Lines and rigs
The line is a key element in successful roach fishing. Lines used for roach are the ultimate in finesse and sensitivity. The line used is from .8 mm to .12 mm.

Sometimes lines as fine as .6 mm or .7 mm can be useful. The floats are sensitive and carrot, pear, or ball-shaped. The latter shape is used primarily where there is a constant current.

The quill and the antenna of the float play an important role. The quill stabilizes the float in the current when there is wind and the water is very deep. A metal antenna is the most sensitive, though more difficult to make out on the water, while glass fiber, carbon, or

Fishing techniques

Groundbaiting

Bank fishing is static. Groundbaiting is necessary to gather the roach. Groundbaits for roach are moderately fine and dark in color. They contain a high proportion of breadcrumbs (brown and white) and sweet, sticky dispersible materials. PV1, treacly copra, fine maize semolina, roast peanuts, fine biscuit and milled hempseed are all basic materials for the preparation of good roach groundbait. Increasingly fishermen are using commercial preparations that have been perfected by the great European champions (including Dasqué, Van Den Eynde, Nudd, Scothorne, Milo…).

Bait

– Bloodworm
This is the king of baits for roach fishing, especially in ponds, slow rivers, and canals. Fragile, the bloodworm can be put on the hook through the head or through the middle.

– Maggot
This very popular bait is easy to obtain and effective for roach. Three types of maggot are used for roach. The gozzer, a large maggot, delicate and fragile, is ideal

for favoring a specific size of fish. Roach of all sizes particularly appreciate the pinkie because it is particularly restless. Finally the caster, an inert bait, a maggot in the course of transformation, is much liked by large roach. These baits are used on a size 12 to about 20 hook.

– Brandling
This is an excellent bait in colored water. It is used on a size 16 to 20 hook. Pastes made at home by the fisherman with flour, sugar solution, coloring, and aromas are excellent for taking roach, particularly in the winter and the spring. Commercial artificial pastes (notably the famous Mystic) are also all effective. A small pellet is placed on a size18 to 22 hook.

– Bread
An excellent bait for roach in winter and at the start of the season. Crumbled, steamed bread made firm with a rolling pin is ideal. A special punch is used to cut the bread which is then put on a size 20 to 22 hook.

– Hempseed
Cooked hempseed is well liked by roach and allows the size of the prey to be chosen.
It is fixed on a fine strong hook with a bronzed or blue shaft.

A roach rig for fishing in rivers and in the current.

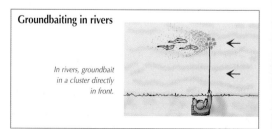

Groundbaiting in rivers

In rivers, groundbait in a cluster directly in front.

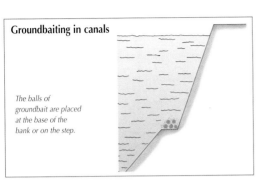

Groundbaiting in canals

The balls of groundbait are placed at the base of the bank or on the step.

A rig for pond fishing.

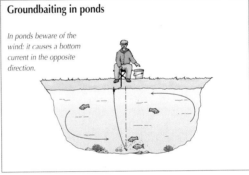

Groundbaiting in ponds

In ponds beware of the wind: it causes a bottom current in the opposite direction.

A canal fishing rig.

– Wheat

This grain is effective for large roach throughout the summer period. The wheat grain is fixed on a size 14 to 16 hook.

Fishing action

The spot chosen is plumbed carefully to enable the angler to establish the depth and nature of the bottom. A clean cast slightly upstream is ideal. Once the groundbait has been moistened and sieved, some live bait can be incorporated (bloodworms, brandlings cut up with scissors) or some grain. Balls the size of an orange are made up and thrown slightly closer than the top section of the rod. A dozen balls will be ample to start fishing.

Once the line is in place, it does not stay still. The banner (the part of the line between the rod tip and the float) must be kept short and tight. Teasing movements are made by moving the float sideways, or even by "pumping" – raising and gently replacing it. This movement is particularly effective in ponds and canals. When there is a bite, the float sinks deep and the strike is made with a small twitch of the rod. The roach is unhooked delicately using a disgorger if necessary. In this way the fish can be returned to the water if it is the end of the fishing session.

ROD-AND-REEL FISHING
Tackle
– The rod

The standard rod measures 13 feet (3.90 m) and has several raised rings to prevent the line from rubbing and sticking to the shaft. It is a carbon rod, very light and perfectly balanced. The sectional type is the most used, telescopic rods being reserved for heavy floats and fishing at long distances.

– The reel

This essential item is either fixed-spool or hooded. There is now a whole range of "special English" reels suited to this kind of fishing and fitted with small capacity spools. The line completely fills the spool, ensuring that casting does not strain the rod.

– Lines and rigs

Bank fishing with rod and reel is typified by the use of special floats. The waggler

is the best known and most used by the majority of fishermen. This float has the line attached below, keeping the banner (the part of the line between the rod tip and the float) below the surface and out of the wind. Increasingly, pre-weighted wagglers are used. This avoids the use of too many weights on the line, an added factor in tangling. There are three basic types of waggler. The straight, fixed waggler is the most used, especially in calm water. There is the fixed bulb waggler, which has a stem and balsa bulb. This type is recommended for reaching great distances and for fishing in the wind. Finally, there is the sliding waggler which is similar but heavier. This can take

up to two or three grams on the line and is used when the depth is more than the length of the rod. Besides wagglers there are two other types of float with the line attached at two points as with those used in pole fishing. These are the "stick" and "Avon" floats. The first is used for fishing close to the bank (up to 45 or 60 feet (15/20 m). The second is mostly used when there is a current, or in rough water. The line used in reel fishing is treated so that it sinks immediately. The line is weighted with pliable leads (SSG, AAA, or BB). This method requires solid, round hooks, sometimes with inturned points. The most used sizes are from size 12 to 22.

ROACH *(Rutilus rutilus)*

"Stick" fishing is well suited to roach fishing in the current.

Groundbaiting
The groundbait for rod-and-reel fishing is heavy and sticky, and may be thrown by hand, but more usually by catapult. For roach the continual use of live animal or vegetable bait instead of groundbait can be effective. This "seeding" can only be carried out at moderate fishing distances (from 45 to 60 feet (15/20 m)). There are some very good commercial groundbaits specially prepared for reel fishing. The standard ingredients for this type of groundbait are gingerbread, husked maize, coarse maize, semolina, roasted peanuts, Holland yellow and, of course, breadcrumbs, sometimes used as a groundbait on its own.

Baits
All animal or vegetable baits used in pole fishing are used in reel fishing. However the maggot is still indispensable to the reel fisherman.

Fishing action
Following plumbing in stages, the line is adjusted so as to skim the bottom. Groundbaiting is carried out with a catapult using medium-sized round balls. Reel fishing is "retrieval" fishing; it is advisable to use a ball of groundbait for each cast. The line is cast from over the shoulder without bringing too much pressure to bear on the rod shaft. When the line reaches the swim, it is braked lightly with one or two fingers on the spool. The line then extends itself perfectly. The rod tip is dipped into the water and a few quick turns of the reel handle will be enough to sink the line. A sharp tug with the rod tip at the surface of the water may be needed to complete the sinking. Once the line is in place and the banner submerged, all that remains is to wait for a bite; some teasing movements can be made with small turns of the reel handle. When there is a bite, the strike is made horizontally, with a definite action.

Waggler rig for roach
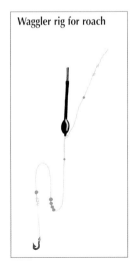

Biology

DESCRIPTION

The bleak (*Alburnus albur-nus*) is a small silvery fish of the cyprinid family much appreciated by the bank fisherman. Its body is thin and elongated. The mouth is upturned, typical of fish that move at the surface. The back is gray-blue or greenish, according to the habitat. The sides and belly are silvery and covered in small, fragile scales that come away easily.

GEOGRAPHIC DISTRIBUTION

This pretty cyprinid is present all over Europe except in some Southern regions.

BEHAVIOR

The bleak breeds in April, May or even June. Its growth is slow and its weight rarely exceeds 3½ ounces (100 g). Gregarious, the bleak swims in large shoals. Depending on the time of day and the amount of light, it likes to seek its food at the surface. Its presence is betrayed by quiet but typical gulping sounds. Its food consists of small mollusks, crustaceans, and land or water insects and vegetable debris.

The bleak likes slow rivers, canals, large lakes, and even running water, provided it is not too cold or muddy.

The bright silvery bleak is a subtle, lively fish, active throughout the year.

The bleak is the ideal fish from which to learn quick reaction with a short rod.

Fishing techniques

Bleak fishing is enjoyed by youngsters and experienced fishermen alike. It is technical, subtle, and fun.

BANK FISHING
Tackle
Bleak fishing is most often carried out close to the bank. For this a telescopic carbon rod is perfect. The length varies between 9 and 12 feet (3–4 m) according to the location. This type of rod has a thin, flexible, solid carbon tip with the line attached. This enables the fish to be lifted straight out of the water. Lines for bleak are extremely light and fine. The line is from .6 mm to .8 mm, often used alone (i.e. without a cast). The floats used are like matchsticks,

carrot, small pear or ball-shaped, with a very short stem. They are balanced to float at the level of the antenna with small shot (size 10 to 13) bunched together. The size 22 to 26 hook is strong yet fine, very sharp, with a long shank.

Groundbait and baits
Groundbaiting is essential for attracting bleak. Its composition should be tasty but not filling. At the same time it should float very well. Types of meal suitable for preparing groundbait for bleak are:

fine brown breadcrumbs, ground biscuit, cornflour, maize flour, dry copra, or roasted peanuts. The unbeatable bait for bleak is bloodworm, especially if it is also used to fortify the groundbait. Pinkies or X-Fise can be used in waters where the bleak are very numerous.

Fishing action
In summer a sunny spot is preferred. The shoals of bleak can be seen with the naked eye. In the winter, calm spots and places where the first rays of the sun fall should be sought. When fishing close to the bank, the groundbait is wetted until it almost becomes a soup: the cloud will last longer. Yellow or white are often appreciated. Taking bleak goes like clockwork. The groundbait is thrown in in pinches so that it bursts in contact with the water. The float is adjusted so that the line moves about close to the surface or in mid-water. The cast is placed in the

Bleak fishing calls for great concentration.

DACE
(LEUSISCUS LEUSISCUS)

BIOLOGY

The dace (*Leuciscus leuciscus*) is a cyprinid frequently confused with the chub. Its body is similar but more thickset than that of the bleak. Its dorsal fin is serrated, the mouth bare, opening beneath a short, rounded snout. The back is gray-green or bluish-gray. The sides are silver and the belly bright and white. Dace spawn from March to May. The female lays about 15,000 to 30,000 eggs on a gravel bottom in shallow water. The gregarious dace likes clear, oxygenated waters. Moreover, it cohabits with salmonids as well as other cyprinids, especially chub and barbel. It is a cautious, very speedy fish. Its food consists of caddis, mollusks, and bloodworms. It is sought by fishermen who livebait for predatory fish.

FISHING TECHNIQUES
Rod fishing

The tackle used for catching roach and bream is the same as that used for dace. A fine, light line is always an advantage. Live baits, particularly maggots scattered with a catapult, are well liked. The dace also has a marked predilection for particle baits, especially hempseed.

Dapping

This itinerant method of fishing is very effective for dace in the summer season.

Tackle
This is reduced to its simplest form and consists of a 15 to 18 foot (5–6 m) telescopic rod. The line is .14 mm to .16 mm line and there is no float. The hook size, from 10 to 18, is suited to the bait used.

Baits
Insects found by the water make the best bait. Grasshoppers, flies, flying ants, crickets, crane flies; these can often be collected on the spot before fishing.

Fishing action
This fishing method combines precision with caution. It is a cross between hunting and fishing. First a shoal of dace is located and noiselessly approached. The bait is dropped as though it had fallen from a tree or a branch. Rather than presenting the bait directly in front of the fish's mouth, it is preferable to slip the insect just behind the dace. The fish turns to snap up the bait and is then pulled out without giving it time to struggle.

cloud of groundbait or close to it. The bite is quick, the float sinking or moving sideways in a flash. A tiny flick of the wrist is enough to hook the fish. Once the fish is unhooked, the bait is replaced on the hook and the line thrown in again. A pinch of groundbait is thrown in with the free hand. These movements, when repeated throughout the fishing session, will soon become reflex...

CHUB
(LEUSISCUS CEPHALUS)

The chub is a gregarious fish with a reputation for greed.

BIOLOGY

The chub (*Leusiscus cephalus*) is a vigorous, widely distributed cyprinid. It has a short, rounded snout and a large head. The mouth is bare with thick, upturned lips, a characteristic of surface fish. The back is brownish-green or bluish. The sides, silvery in young specimens, are old gold or gray in larger fish. The belly is a bright white or gray-yellow. Chub may vary in size from 8 to 16 inches (20–40 cm). Some specimens may reach 24 or 28 inches (60 or 70 cm)

with a weight of 11 to 13 pounds (5–6 kg). The chub is widespread throughout Europe.

The spawning season of the chub is between April and June. The female lays up to 100,000 eggs on a gravel bottom. Chub are gregarious and like lively, oxygenated waters. This cyprinid is legendary among fishermen for its greed. An omnivore, it feeds on animal and vegetable baits, even meat or cheese.

FISHING TECHNIQUES

The chub bites all the year round. All methods of groundbait fishing with pole or rod and reel are suitable. Only the type of bait changes with the seasons. If the chub is keen on classic baits such as maggots, bloodworms, casters, or particle baits, it also shows a particular taste for more original baits. In the autumn, fruit (grapes, cherries, etc.) or ripe berries are acceptable. Baiting on size 2 to 14 hooks is delicate. It is sometimes necessary to use a small needle to thread the fruit on without ruining it. During the winter months the chub is attracted by blood, meat, and offal. Although poultry blood is the most effective, it is most often replaced by bovine blood put to congeal in a cool place. A cube of blood is placed on a size 6 to16 hook. Meat, pâté, and sausage are also typical chub-fishing baits. Cocktail sausages are practical and effective, threaded loosely by means of a needle onto a size 6 to 8 treble hook. Small pieces of raw meat, especially beef, can be used on a size 10 to 12 hook. As regards pâté, the best is ham pâté, cut into cubes and used on a 6 to 10 hook. Chub, especially large ones, mount an appreciable defense so the use of rod and reel is preferable. The bite of the chub is fast and deep. At the start, as soon as it feels the hook, it invariably puts up a tough fight. It should be kept in check as

soon as it is hooked; if not, it tends to head for the opposite bank or the nearest snag.

Chub fishing is practiced throughout the seasons.

BARBEL
(BARBUS BARBUS)

BIOLOGY

Description

The barbel (*Barbus barbus*) is a powerful combative cyprinid. It is readily recognizable by its long, cylindrical body. Its belly is flat, the head conical and the dorsal fin very serrated. Below the snout the toothless mouth has thick lips. The upper lip is provided with four long barbels that serve as organs of touch and taste. The first ray of the dorsal fin is thick, rigid, and toothed. The back is brown or gray-green. The sides are pale, copper, or ocher, the belly yellow or whitish.

Geographic distribution

The barbel is present in numerous central European rivers, as far as the Black Sea.

Behaviour

The spawning season of the barbel is from May to July. The female lays about 8,000 eggs in the current on a sandy bottom. The barbel is a gregarious fish that prefers clear, running, well-oxygenated water. It lives equally well in large rivers and in the rapid, cold waters of salmon rivers. A bottom feeding fish, the barbel turns over stones and pebbles with its powerful snout. Its food consists of chironomes (bloodworms), ephemera, and trichoptera, as well as plants and zooplankton.

FISHING TECHNIQUES

Floating line
Materials
– *Rod*
A ringed telescopic rod 15 to 18 ft (5 to 6 m) long of the "Bologna" type is right for this kind of fishing. The rings should be raised to prevent the line from sticking to the rod shaft.

– *Reel*
A modest reserve of line suffices. A skirted or fixed-spool reel loaded with .16 to .18 mm line is fine.

– *Rig*
This consists of either a stubby ball- or pear-shaped float with a large stem, or an Avon type attached at two points, which resists disturbance by the current. This float is balanced with large shot grouped together.

A ringed rod and a reel are advisable to overcome that tough adversary, the barbel.

The hook is round, or round with an inturned point and a shank suited to the bait used.

Groundbaiting and baits

Though fond of groundbait, the barbel is easily satisfied. The best way of groundbaiting is to use live or vegetable bait cast in by hand or with a catapult. Maggots, hempseed, casters (maggot pupae), and wheat are most suitable for this type of groundbaiting. As far as baits are concerned, besides those mentioned above, the barbel particularly likes mayfly larvae, collected on sandy bottoms with a fine mesh net.

Fishing action

The ideal place to catch barbel is in a clear river with a steady current flowing over gravel beds. Groundbaiting is carried out by throwing in bait or grain by hand or with a catapult. The line is held with the banner taut, avoiding too much restraint so it drifts naturally in the current. The bite is deep and decisive. When hooked, the barbel shakes its head, putting up a fierce defense. The rod must be held high to keep in touch with the fish. When tired, the barbel is brought to the net on the surface. Care must be taken to ensure it does not attempt a last-minute escape.

Legering

This is a most effective method of catching large barbel. The tackle and method are the same as those used for bream or tench. However, a feeder filled with live bait (maggots) is more effective than one filled with groundbait.

Biology

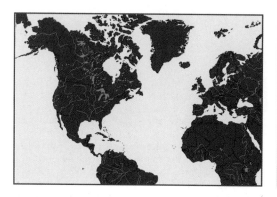

FOREIGN NAMES

French: anguille.
German: Aal.
Spanish: anguilla.

DESCRIPTION

The eel is readily recognizable by its elongated serpentine form covered in abundant mucus. Minute scales appear toward the age of three years.

The eel's thick, slimy skin gives it the power to capture atmospheric oxygen and thus move about by wriggling over wet ground. The pectoral fins are inserted behind the gill openings. There are no ventral fins and the dorsal and anal fins meet at the end of the body. The mouth has hard lips and the jaws have small, fine teeth. The eyes are small and the tiny gill openings are close to the pectoral fins. Two pairs of nostrils situated in front of the eyes on the end of the snout open into a highly-developed ophthalmic chamber that plays an important role in the eel's sense of smell.

Depending on the species, the eel can have a narrow head or a wide flattened skull. Before it leaves the salt water, the young eel is transparent, then becomes opaque and acquires dark patches. These become more and more plentiful until the final coloring is achieved. The back is greenish-brown, lighter at the sides and the belly is white or yellowish. These colors are more or less accentuated according to the individual, going from dark brown-

The eel with its serpentine shape is surrounded by mystery.

EEL *(Anguilla anguilla)*

The eel's ability to crawl enables it to travel considerable distances.

green to light green. When the breeding fish descend to the sea, the back becomes darker and marbled with brown-red, and the belly is silver-white, hence the name silver eel.

GEOGRAPHIC DISTRIBUTION

In the Northern Hemisphere there are two species: the European eel (*Anguilla anguilla*), widespread throughout Europe, and the American eel (*Anguilla rostrata*), present on the east coast of America.

BEHAVIOR

The eel is a carnivorous migratory catadromous fish; in other words, it lays its eggs in the sea and spends the rest of its life in rivers. Its habitat is very varied: marine environments, brackish zones, and most fresh waters. Its ability to crawl and survive short spells out of water enables it to move about between ponds and ditches in wet areas. It only avoids waters that are very cold, and high altitude streams.

Diet

The feeding of the eel changes according to its age and the environment it finds itself in. The adult is omnivorous with carnivorous tendencies. Aquatic invertebrates, crustaceans, molluscs, worms, frogs and toads, and fish all form part of its diet. It likes dead prey and feeds mainly during the night.

Reproduction

The reproduction of the eel is still surrounded by mystery and question marks. Thanks to the work of the Danish oceanographer, Johannes Schmidt (1877--1933) we now know the approximate location of the eel's breeding ground. This is in the Sargasso Sea off the east coast of the United States. The Sargasso Sea has the peculiarity of being influenced by strong currents and is covered by a dense mat of weeds. Reproduction starts in the autumn and the eel arrives at its destination at the beginning of spring (February–March). Spawning takes place at a great depth (1200 feet/400 m). Each female lays about 1 million eggs which hatch in a month into transparent larvae, leptocephales. In the course of a two- or three-year journey the Gulf Stream and its side streams carry them close to the American and European coasts. The larvae undergo transformation and stop feeding. At this time the elvers are subjected to heavy, often completely illegal fishing. Tons of elvers are taken and exported to the Iberian peninsula and to Asiatic countries, whose inhabitants are passionately fond of them. According to the scientists this intensive fishing may well compromise the future of the species.

Fishing techniques

Fishing techniques have evolved over the passage of time, but traditional methods are still firmly established. Eel can be taken on a worm-ball and by legering.

It is not unusual to catch a large eel when legering.

LEGERING

Legering is currently the most commonly used method of catching large eels.

Tackle

This is very simple. A solid ringed rod of the type used in livebaiting for pike is perfectly suitable. A fixed-spool casting or medium-sized reel makes up the basic equipment. This is filled to the lip of the spool with tough .30 to .40 mm line. The rig is made up with a round or flat olive of ½ to 1 ounce (15–30 g) up against a stop weight (size SSG or BB). Equally effective is a small length of plastic tubing inserted to protect the knot between the line and the cast. The cast is attached to the main line by a swivel clip. The cast is very supple, and composed of some 12 to 15 inches (30–40 cm) of .25 to .30 mm line and provided with a simple

BURBOT

BIOLOGY

There is an American variety of the burbot. Larger than the European variety, it can attain a weight of 11 to 13 pounds (5–6 kg) at a length of 3 feet (1 m). This fish is found in North America, especially in Alaska and Canada. It is much sought after because of its delicate flesh.

FISHING TECHNIQUES

The burbot can be caught on the leger by the same method as for the European fish. However, it is a more aggressive fish and will not refuse a fresh dead bait on the line. Another effective way of catching burbot is with a lure – a waggling spoon being particularly effective. Native fishermen use this method to catch them under the ice.

The eel is often difficult to unhook.

Fishing techniques

Once hooked, the eel puts up a wild defense.

solid hook from size 0 to 5, according to the bait used. When fishing for very big eels, a steel or Kevlar braid trace is used instead of nylon. A float is not necessary, but is infinitely more exciting when the eel takes the bait.

Baits

The eel is an omnivore. Earthworms, a bunch of brandlings or large maggots, and cooked mussels, and are all first-rate baits. Shelled crayfish tail or a small dead fish (bleak, minnow, small roach) left on the bottom are very effective baits for luring the largest eels.

Fishing action

The ideal is to fish at night, which is not always possible because of regulations: by day, a cluttered spot is good (dead trees, snags of any kind) close to a bridge or a large backwash. Water colored by a storm is a godsend for taking a "boxful" of eels. The cast is kept mainly on the bottom. The eel bite is characteristic: a few tugs at the outset, then the float goes right down, heading for open water. The pick-up is opened to release a little line, then a hard strike is made. To unhook the eel, it is best to put it on a sheet of newspaper and use a pair of stout pliers.

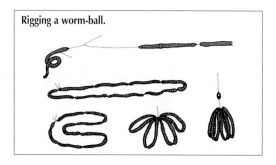

Rigging a worm-ball.

BURBOT

BIOLOGY

The burbot is a member of the order Gadiformes. Its slimy skin is covered in tiny scales. The flattened head has a wide mouth with fine teeth. A single barbel decorates the lower jaw. Its color varies from ocher yellow marbled with violet-gray or greenish brown. The belly is yellowish or whitish-gray. Its size varies from 8 to 10 inches (20–25 cm) on average and may reach 30 inches (75 cm). The burbot likes to live in medium and large European rivers, also in the great alpine lakes.

It breeds in the winter from December to January and lays up to 1 million minute eggs. Its nocturnal habits are not favorable for fishing. However, it can be caught when the water is muddy and colored, and the weather is gloomy.

The burbot has a single barbel under its lower jaw.

The burbot, a rare fish, is known for its nocturnal habits.

FISHING TECHNIQUES

The tackle and leger used for the eel are perfectly suitable for the burbot. The bait should rest on the bottom. The bite of the turbot is unspectacular. The fish swallows the bait right down and allows itself to be brought in without making much defense. Little fished for and not well known by fishermen, the burbot is sought for the excellence of its flesh and of its liver, which are much prized by gourmets.

The burbot always swallows the bait deep inside.

A HUNTING CYPRINID: THE ASP

The asp is a carnivorous cyprinid that can be caught with all types of lure.

Aspius aspius, the asp (aspe in French, Rapfen in German) is one of the very rare carnivores belonging to the large cyprinid family. In Europe it is the only true fish-eating member of the family; carp, and chub in particular occasionally include small fish in their diet.

BIOLOGY

The asp is a beautiful, slender flat-sided fish with projecting jaws. The back is bluish-green in color and the sides are silver and the belly white. To fishermen not familiar with it, it looks like a giant bleak. A characteristic feature is a well-developed anal fin with a markedly concave outer border. The fish may reach nearly 3 feet in length, with a weight of 17 to 22 pounds (8–10 kg). The young feed on invertebrates (worms, insects, crustaceans, and mollusks),

but very quickly turn to prey on the alevins of other cyprinid species. Starting from about 8 or 12 inches (20–30 cm), the species is almost exclusively piscivorous. As with almost all the cyprinids, the asp lives and, remarkably, hunts in shoals whose members are pretty well the same sizes. Even the large specimens hunt in organized packs, cornering their prey before launching an attack. Roach and bleak are among their favorite prey. The species likes running water in the rivers of central Europe. Exceptionally it adapts to the great lakes. The original European zone of distribution extended from the Elbe to the Ural, including all the great river basins emptying north into the Baltic (Vistula), or south into the Black Sea and the Caspian (Danube, Dneiper, Volga). Small populations also existed in Scandinavia (in south Sweden and Finland). In 1958 and later, the species was introduced into the Rhine basin where it is now fairly well spread. Spawning takes place in April and May over beds of gravel or pebbles swept by a fairly strong current. Growth is rapid and the young attain a size of 6 to 8 inches (15–20 cm) within a year, and a length of 16 to 20 inches (40–50 cm) by the end of the third year.

FISHING TECHNIQUES

A carnivore that hunts primarily at the surface, the asp is caught by casting lures and flies. The lures (spoons, spinners, plug baits, and flexible lures) should be small and imitate little foraging fish. By contrast, since it is often necessary to cast a good distance (mid-current in big rivers) the rod and reel should be quite powerful. Nylon of .22 and .26 mm, or better still .15 to .20 mm braided polythene make possible the necessary long casts with small lures, and are strong enough to control a good fish. For fly-fishing it is advisable to use a boat so as to be able to present bright streamers in the chosen spots. The asp has a fairly tender, membranous mouth: the fisherman should never be brutal with it.

The asp is one of the rare truly carnivorous cyprinids, a typical inhabitant of the Rhine, in Europe and eastern Europe.

Glossary

Amphibiotic: a term applied to a fish with a development cycle that takes place partly in fresh water and partly in sea water.

Anadromous: a term applied to a fish that goes up a river from the sea to spawn (see potamodromous).

Benthic: an adjective describing animals and plants that live on the bottom of lakes and oceans (the benthos).

Benthophage: a term applied to bottom-feeding fish. The gudgeon, a cyprinid, is an insectivorous benthophage.

Bolognese technique: a fishing technique, originated and developed by the Italians, which uses a long rod with rings, a reel, and a floating line.

Bottom-feeding fish: a term applied to a fish that searches the bottom for food.

Catadromous: a term applied to a fish that goes down to the sea to spawn (synonym: thalassotomous).

Catch and release: fishing without killing. The fish is held in a keep net, before being returned to the water.

Chironomid: generic term applied to the larvae of various families of two-winged flies (Diptera), but usually to midges. These larvae are customarily known by fishermen as bloodworms.

Dangling: a line-fishing technique in which the fish is attracted by making the bait pass to and fro in front of it.

Downstream migration: mass movement of fish down a watercourse.

Enticement: the act of manipulating a bait to make it more attractive to the fish.

Hooking: the taking of a lure or bait by a fish.

Gregarious: a term applied to species whose members live in groups. Most herbivorous and omnivorous coarse fish are gregarious.

Ichthyophage: feeding on fish (adjective: ichthyophagous).

Lucifuge: a term applied to a fish that shuns light.

Pelagic: a term applied to fish that live in the deepest parts of waters.

Pool: a calm, deep part of a river, between two currents. Salmon position themselves in pools to rest before continuing the journey to their spawning grounds.

Potamodromous: a term applied to a fish that migrates, for example between feeding and spawning grounds, while remaining in fresh water (compare with anadromous).

Protractile: capable of being protruded or extended. Some herbivorous and omnivorous coarse fish have protractile lips.

Rattail: a tapering succession of nylon sections of decreasing diameter in a fishing line.

Recovery: winding in the line on the fishing reel.

Rod action: a term applied to the "responsiveness" of a rod. A distinction is drawn between stiff rods (tip action) and flexible rods, which bend throughout their length (parabolic action).

Slackening: halting the drift of a line in the current, in order to recover the bait and attract the attention of the fish.

Striking: the action of the rod by which the fish is hooked.

Spawning: the laying of eggs by female fish, followed by their fertilization by the male.

Spawning ground: the place where fish lay their eggs.

Waders: a waterproof garment combining boots and trousers, worn by anglers standing in the river.

Wading: Fishing when standing in the river, wearing waders.

Whirl: a round ripple indicating that a fish is feeding at the surface.

Waggler: the basic float for the British fishing technique; it is a feature of the waggler that it is attached to the line only at the base.

Index

Pages numbers in Roman script refer to running text; numbers in *italic* script to boxed text; numbers printed in **bold** indicate that the section is a broader treatment of the subject

Index

Photographic credits